FRONT PAGE

Covers of the
Twentieth Century

First published in Great Britain in 2003 by Weidenfeld & Nicolson
© Weidenfeld & Nicolson

All rights reserved. No part of this publication may be reproduced, stored in a retrieval system, or transmitted in any form or by any means, electronic, mechanical, photocopying,
recording, or otherwise, without the prior permission of both the copyright owner and the
above publisher of this book.

A CIP catalogue record for this book is available from the British Library.
ISBN 02978 2971 8
Printed in Spain
Weidenfeld & Nicolson

The Orion Publishing Group Ltd
Orion House
5 Upper Saint Martin's Lane
London, WC2H 9EA

FRONT PAGE

Covers of the
Twentieth Century

TEXTS

Stéphane Duperray and Raphaële Vidaling

With the collaboration of
Cécile Amara, Agnieszka Ples and Alain-Xavier Wurst

IMAGES GALORE

These days magazines tend to use their covers to advertise their interior. Headlines, sub-titles, advertisements and lists of contents jostle together where once the image reigned supreme. Of course there is always an image there still in the background. It's hard to know sometimes who this strategy serves. Does it reassure the reader by telling them exactly what lies inside? Or do the editors of the magazine feel happier when all of its wares are on display?

For a long time though, things were different. The image alone was trusted much more. As a result every magazine cover was a work in its own right, a subtle mixture of art and marketing, reflecting a spirit rather than a menu or a table of contents. And the art director was king.

We have sought to assemble a collection of covers that speak through images: the most beautiful, the most striking, those that represent a genre, era, country or artistic current the best. We have deliberately left out specialised magazines, particularly art or graphics magazines. Instead we have sought artistic prowess in general interest periodicals: *Paris-Match, The Sunday*

Telegraph Magazine, Picture Post, Life. We have of course included thematic magazines, like *Lui* or *Fortune,* because apart from their subject matter (in these cases eroticism and business respectively), they show a true care for aesthetic quality. Many of our choices could simply not have been ignored, so essential were they in cradling the dreams of artists everywhere, whether contributing to them or inspired by them: *Esquire, Vogue, Harper's Bazaar, The New Yorker, Vu.* Other, less known ones, like *Il Borghese* or *Simplicissimus* struck us through the originality and quality of their graphics.

But where to start with such a vast corpus which covers the entire Western world with a timeline encompassing the 19th and the 20th centuries? We felt our way, exploring as we went. We never intended to be either exhaustive or objective in our research. For this is an anthology which is full of gaps and favourites. Two places opened their doors to us: the Musée d'Histoire de la Presse and the American Library in Paris. We sent our picture researcher through miles of shelves. Through tons of archives and thousands of boxes. What did she have but chance to guide her in her choices? She had an eye for quality, an essential skill when it came to choosing between this image or that, the pink rather than the blue, Sophia Loren rather than Katharine Hepburn. The choice was difficult, often arbitrary, always guided by visual pleasure and sometimes constrained by material impossibilities such as ruined covers, bindings overlapping the edges and missing issues.

This is a book that has been produced backwards. First the images, then the text, with much attention paid to the layout. It was the least we could do in homage to these pioneers of press graphics. Once we had selected all of the covers we then had to organise them. We wanted to preserve the startling, striking aspect of many of them, but we also had so much to say!

So finally the book was split into two parts. First a selection of magazines, each one presented on one or two double pages using a range of covers from different periods, accompanied by an explanatory text giving an historical overview. The second part of the book groups together covers by theme, whether artistic movement, personality or event. The issue here was a comparative rather than a historical one, from the many faces of Marilyn to the changing image of De Gaulle or Churchill, from the influence of art deco on magazines to that of pop art.

Don't bother looking for the missing covers. There are far too many of them. That we are well aware of. And we really are sorry. But those that are included suffice to prove one thing, that behind the history of magazines appears history itself, both political and social, as well as the history of art, because photographers, painters, illustrators, poster and advertising artists often belong to the same world. Yet this younger sister of galleries and museums, the Press, has only been able to get onto the streets and into people's homes thanks to two key players who are often ignored: the often unknown graphic designers who have made these visuals so accessible, and the hundreds of thousands of vendors, whose kiosks enable all of these wonderful images to become so easily available. We would like to address a special thanks to them. And to everyone else. Enjoy your trip through time!

CONTENTS

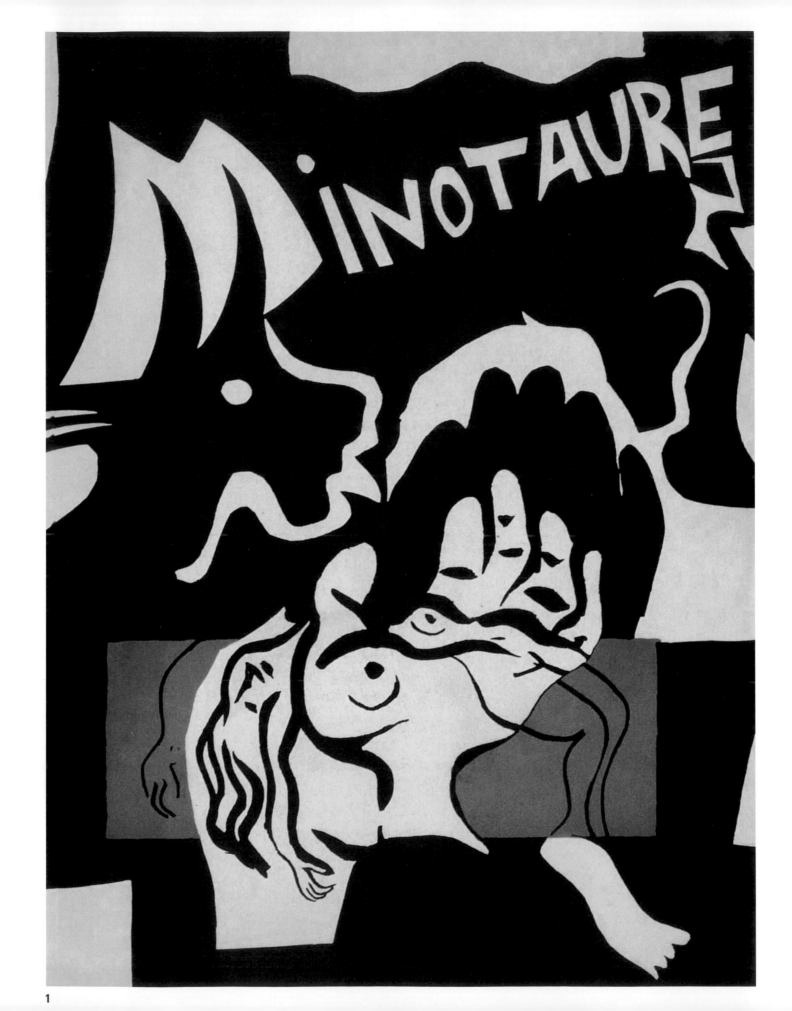

1

A SHORT HISTORY
OF CLASSIC COVERS

The history of magazine covers is a relatively short one, barely two centuries long, but rich in developments nevertheless. Although this history is closely linked to that of the press in general, it has some unique characteristics. The development of printing techniques has not evolved in the same way as the reproduction of illustrations, while artistic movements or photography have had less influence on daily newspapers than on the magazine press and its covers.

The expansion of the press started in the West at the end of the 18th century; public opinion could be expressed for the very first time. The movement that led to the independence of the United States was one of its first historical effects. The irrepressible rise of the press during the following century was the result of several factors, including political liberalism and the industrial revolution. No caricature-wielding political journals would have been possible without freedom of expression and no large-scale circulation without the modern printing press.

At the end of the 19th century the press became the uncontested fourth estate in the democratic and industrialised countries of Europe and the United States. It had a monopoly on information, as well as forming opinion and directing fashions. Thanks to the increasing literacy of the masses and the cuts in prices which resulted from the industrialisation of printing and the introduction of advertising, daily papers became common consumer products. Complementing the daily press, the magazine press increased its diversity and circulation. Its covers stood out through the use of colour, the work of reputed artists and eventually photography. This was the apogee of the written press, with the establishment of powerful groups such as Hearst in the United States, Beaverbrook in the United Kingdom or Prouvost in France.

The third stage commenced with the loss of the monopoly of the printed press through the growth of radio in the 1930s, and above all television in the 1950s-60s. The daily press was the worst hit, although effects varied according to country. In Great Britain, and Northern Europe in general, circulation was virtually unaffected by these new media. In France, the national daily press collapsed in favour of magazines and, to a lesser extent, regional dailies.

Magazines had to adapt to these new conditions amid stiff competition, or risk falls in circulation. The widespread use of photography and colour, both on the cover and inside, were the two major developments. As the press became ever more specialised, it was obliged to build up a detailed knowledge of its readership and use increasingly sophisticated marketing techniques. Magazine covers were painstakingly designed and produced. It has indeed been proven that the impact of a cover can have a dramatic effect on sales. Today, more than ever, adapting to a shifting marketplace is the key to survival.

The Emergence of the Magazine Press in the 19th Century

The benchmark was set by the British in the early 19th century. With the founding of *The Times* in 1785, followed shortly by a host of other dailies, Great Britain enjoyed the greatest freedom of expression in Europe. There was subtle censorship though, since the large stamp duties imposed until the 1840s, high printing and purchase prices meant that readership was limited essen-

THE INDIAN CHILD.—See Poem on Page 2.

tially to the upper classes. The first magazines started to appear around this time. Their founders were not yet aware of the considerable interest that a cover might have for a reader, with resulting increases in sales. *Blackwood's,* founded in Edinburgh in 1817 and which survived until 1980, kept the same cover from issue to issue, depicting George Buchanan, a 16th century Scottish historian and scholar, a character of limited appeal.

The covers of *Strand,* the magazine that serialised the adventures of Sherlock Holmes, always showed the same street scene. Their only great innovation was to replace the horse-drawn carriages with cars once the former had disappeared. The first six issues of *Punch* each had a different cover, but the seventh was such a success that it was kept for nearly a century.

Stamp duty also existed in France and political censorship was heavier. One way of getting round it, however, was to publish illustrations that expressed what could not be written. Launched by the illustrator and caricaturist Philipon in 1830, *Le Charivari,* for which Daumier would contribute illustrations, and *La Caricature,* initiated the French tradition of the satirical political magazine. Along with Honoré Daumier, André Gill was the star illustrator who sketched celebrities of the period, including Balzac, Hugo, Zola, Napoléon III, Garibaldi and Bismarck.

These illustrations were a source of permanent conflict with the censors who frequently fined or imposed bans on the magazines that published them. In contrast, the caricatures of the English satirical magazine *Punch* were less virulent, perhaps due to a more tranquil political scene.

International Illustrations

In 1842 Herbert Ingram realised that not only could images attract a large public but that there was also a market for a general news weekly. He therefore launched the *Illustrated London News.* The success was immediate and the formula was copied the following year in France with *L'Illustration,* in Germany with *Die Illustrierte Zeitung* and in Spain with *la Ilustracion* in 1849. *Harper's Weekly* was founded in the United States in 1857 and the *Vsemirnaia Illiustratsiia* in Russia in 1869.

L'Illustration and its competitors were the preserve of a rich clientele. Covers and illustrations were more aesthetic or educational than satirical. Gustave Doré was one of the leading illustrators of these magazines. In 1866 the print run of *L'Illustration* was 18,000 copies, compared with the 33,000 of its competitor *Le Monde Illustré.* The latter was cheaper since it shared the cost of illustrations with *The Illustrated London News* and *Die Illustrierte Zeitung;* they published the same images.

But as far as the quality both of its articles and its images were concerned *L'Illustration* was the most prestigious French magazine of this period. In 1879 it became the first to publish photographs. Representing the wealthy, republican and enlightened bourgeoisie, it was politically to the right, although this did not prevent it from supporting Baudelaire's *Fleurs du Mal* after his death. The circulation of *L'Illustration* kept on rising, reaching 400,000 copies for certain special issues published during the First World War.

Across the Atlantic, *Harper's Weekly* had reached 160,000 copies by 1872. At a time when the American population was no larger than that of Great Britain or France, this high circulation can be explained by the fact that there were no major national newspapers in the United States. The magazine press played an even more important role there than in Europe. *Harper's Weekly* was less elitist than its European equivalents and published the political sketches of Thomas Nast, a fervent partisan of Lincoln and the Republicans. It is to Nast whom we owe the famous depiction of Uncle Sam that has been reproduced, tweaked and mutated in thousands of ways ever since.

The birth of these widely circulated illustrated magazines is closely linked to technical advances in printing. In 1816 the cylinder press was invented; this enabled both sides of a page to be printed in a single operation, and brought printing rates up to 1,000 pages an hour. In the 1840s-1850s this soared to 20,000 pages and soon to 50,000 with the invention of the rotary press in 1876.

The Lithographic Revolution in France

Lithography was the key to the growth of illustrations and it all started in France. In 1815 the Comte de Lasteyrie, the son-in-law of La Fayette, started to use the lithographic process. This technique facilitated the reproduction of illustrations. Lithography's press debut came in 1834, with the publication of a drawing in *Le Charivari.* By 1882 it took just two days to produce an illustration, compared with a week in 1872. Around 1890 the improvement of lithographic printing led to a widespread use of colour illustrations. This was the period of Toulouse-Lautrec. In 1904 the offset process was invented in the United States. It is still used today for most publications.

Press for the French People

In the second half of the 19th century, press readership widened considerably. Technology enabled large print runs while advertising brought prices down, the authorities relaxed their control of the press, growing urbanisation facilitated circulation and the increasing literacy of the population created a potential market. All that remained was to develop a popular press. In 1863 Moïse-Polydore Millaud founded *Le Petit Journal* with the philosophy of 'Let us have the courage to be stupid.' He himself hardly knew how to read but realised that the lower classes could only be reached through reduced prices and sensationalism. The success was phenomenal. In 1886 *Le Petit Journal* was the first publication in the world to sell a million copies.

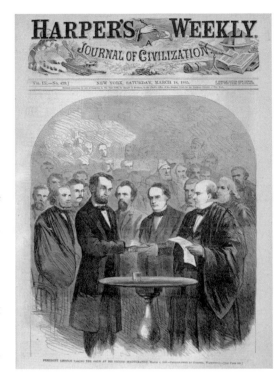

3

4

In 1884 its illustrated supplement was launched with a colour picture on the first and last page. Its competitors rushed to imitate it. The French expression from this era 'le sang à la une' or 'blood in the headlines' gives an idea of the kind of illustrations that sold copies.

The educated public, for whom all press had been aimed at up until this time, put up with tiny print and texts without titles. There was no commercial aspect to the layout since newspapers and magazines were only available upon subscription or in cafés, clubs, libraries and the like.

With the development of sales through kiosks or by street vendors, images and big headlines became essential to attract potential buyers. The famous 'J'accuse' of Zola in 1898, or rather of Clemenceau since it was he who had had the idea for this shock title, would never have had the same impact if it had been published twenty years earlier.

New Kinds of Magazines

It was around this time that fashion magazines made their appearance, exporting their French-influenced drawings and designs all over the world. Changes in the social role of women were now gathering apace.

In 1908 the Parisian couturier Paul Poiret introduced the long and slim feminine silhouette. This new style which prefigured that of the 1920s would be popularised by Erté, who worked both for Poiret and as an illustrator for fashion magazines before emigrating to America. *Gil Blas* was a rather sophisticated men's magazine, where writers such as Guy de Maupassant were published. In France an act of parliament of July 1881 gave total freedom to the press. The first magazines to benefit were the purveyors of political satire. However, *Le Charivari* lost ground to *L'Assiette au Beurre*. Every week, from 1901 to 1914, this magazine with anarchist tendencies published sixteen pages of ferocious caricature covering the society of the Belle Époque (1890-1914). Contributors included Caran d'Ache, Steinlen and Robida.

Le Rire is the best example of magazines which were more humorous than satirical and of lighter rather than political content. Founded in 1894 *Le Rire* was a sixteen-page weekly; four pages contained colour illustrations, adverts for condoms and impotency remedies or even erotic photographs.

Toulouse-Lautrec was the most famous contributor to the journal, while Swiss artist Steinlen was the most prolific, producing more than 2,000 illustrations for 50 publications between 1883 and 1900.

The Golden Age of Fine Arts

The dawn of photography marked the zenith of press illustrators who were producing covers of exceptional quality. There was no separation, as would be the case later, between artists producing art for art's sake, and simple illustrators providing commercial products. In the United States illustrators such as Norman Rockwell, would raise this form of expression to the highest level by making it their speciality. In Europe, particularly France, magazine illustration often served as a springboard and breadwinner for young artists such as Bonnard.

The greatest painters never hesitated to contribute to the prestige and circulation of magazines, while art directors were also responsible for launching new artistic movements. *Jugendstil*, the German version of Art Nouveau, owed its name to the magazine

5

6

7

8

Jugend. And during its short life (1893-1895), *L'Estampe originale* benefited from contributors that included Pissarro, Gauguin, Renoir, Signac, Vallotton and Toulouse-Lautrec, who drew the first cover.

For the first time ever, art and artistic exploration were brought within reach of the general public; magazines showcased every new art movement, from the Cubism of Léger to the Surrealism of Dalí, not forgetting Art Deco. Such movements were major influences on professional illustrators and poster artists such as Cassandre in the 1930s. Certain journals considered themselves the representatives of specific artistic movements; in the case of *Minotaure,* Surrealism. With covers by Picasso, Duchamp, Miró, Matisse, Magritte, Ernst and many others, *Minotaure,* published five times a year between 1933 and 1939, was the last representative of French artistic predominance before the Second World War.

Logos, typography and page layout were also influenced by artistic movements. The Art Nouveau style that flourished between 1890 and 1910 was echoed in numerous magazines. Some even kept the style into the 1930s. Art Nouveau was largely superseded by Art Deco, which was exported successfully to the United States through magazines. The influence of modernism and Bauhaus started to make itself felt just before the Second World War. Page layouts became less crowded, less fancy and started using simpler, straighter fonts like Helvetica.

Photography Rings the Changes

In 1889 there were 1,747 magazines being published in Paris. In 1900 the United States counted 5,000, with 50 boasting a print-run of over 100,000, where in 1860 there had been only 500. The magazine press, premier source of entertainment in the absence of radio and cinema, was in its heyday. The technical progress which had enabled these impressive print runs would oblige the press to adapt to innovations.

9

10

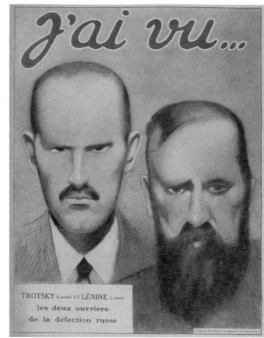

11

12

In use from the 1880s, half-tone gravure enabled photographs to be printed by breaking down the image into dots of varying sizes. In the years preceding the Great War the press put photography on its front pages. But there was a problem. Although information could be sent by telegraph (1832) then telephone (1876), photographs could only be sent by horse, by rail or by steamer. Therefore, photography was initially used much more in magazines than in daily newspapers, since the latter obviously could not wait longer than a few hours for a photograph. In 1917 Édouard Belin developed the belinograph, a precursor of the fax machine, which enabled photographs to be sent across the telephone network. The conditions were then right for a revolution in the press.

A number of new publications were born during the war. Some of those that did not indulge in brainwashing even survived hostilities. *Le Crapouillot* aimed to be a non-conformist paper written by soldiers. *Le Canard Enchaîné,* an anticlerical and anti-militarist left-wing daily, denounced cowards and war profiteers. From 1915 to 1918, *La Baïonnette,* a satirical journal quite representative of the period, published various anti-German sketches.

Extremism, Literature and Photomontage

During the inter-war period radical politics emerged. The rise of totalitarian movements, first Communist, then Fascist and Nazi engendered a new kind of political weekly. In France, Sennep, Jean Eiffel and Poulbot maintained the tradition of the political caricature, although it was reduced in size and returned to black and white in order to leave more room for texts that were often excessive but produced by brilliant polemicists and writers. This involvement in political debate by high level intellectuals encouraged publishing houses to launch periodicals that were almost all text. The ancestor of these publications was *La Libre Parole,* an anti-Semitist journal founded at the time of the Dreyfus Affair. The publisher Arthème Fayard opened hostilities in 1924 with *Candide,* followed by *Je suis partout* in 1930, a publication which was even more right-wing, under the editorship of Robert Brasillach. Gallimard responded with *Marianne* in 1932, joining other left-wing publications like *Vendredi.* These weeklies either disappeared or else slipped into collaboration after the occupation of France.

The Communist Party had launched its own organ *Regards* in 1932. Aragon wrote for this journal, which saw itself as an illustrated weekly for the working class, inventing class photography to combat the bourgeois image. Imported from the USSR, the new technique of photomontage, which lent itself well to propaganda, was systematically used for cover art. The greatest names in photography, such as Robert Capa or

Henri Cartier-Bresson, worked for *Regards,* a magazine whose aesthetic policy was original and innovative.

Innovation in the United States

After the First World War, Europe had been bled dry, both literally and figuratively. Artistic movements continued to flourish, but it was the dynamism of the American economy and society which would now engender major innovations in the press.

The homogeneity of the American market and the capitalist dynamic created ideal conditions for the formation of huge press groups that were often created by a single man with a strong, even megalomaniac personality. In 1935 William Randolph Hearst's group employed 15,000 people, published nine magazines and twenty daily papers.

These groups aimed for profitability and made the most of the latest marketing techniques. The intuition of a great press magnate, the benefit of a market study and a well-orchestrated launch can work wonders. In 1923 Henry Luce and Britton Hadden launched a new magazine formula which would use short articles to summarise most of the news that a hurried reader should know.

Time was the first news magazine, a genre that would cross the Atlantic only after the war. In 1929 it breached the 200,000 copy barrier. The covers of *Time,* which generally illustrate the main subject of the magazine, are not particularly original. Yet the 'Man of the Year' who illustrates the last cover of December is nevertheless reported on by the world's media.

Then in 1929 Henry Luce launched *Fortune,* a journal aimed at the business elite, and whose covers have been among the most artistic in American magazine history.

The Golden Age of Photojournalism

During the 1930s more and more households became equipped with radios. At first, newspapers refused to carry listings of radio programmes, fearing that if the

13

14

15

16

new medium became too popular then their sales would suffer. In fact the two media never really competed with each other. *Time* even produced the programme *Time Marches On.* Newspaper and magazine circulation continued to increase, but publications had to adapt and find ways of complementing radio. Increased and better use of photography was one such tactic. The public was naturally interested in photographs of places, people and events that they had only ever heard or read about. In addition, the development of lighter weight and more effective cameras enabled pictures to be taken quickly, with much reduced exposure times and without the subject even realising they were being photographed. With the advent of the Leica 35mm 1925 model, photojournalism was born. *Life* was launched by Henry Luce in 1936. The formula consisted of publishing photographic reportages on a wide variety of subjects. Yet text was not neglected since the work of

the best journalists and writers was also used. The idea was copied in France with *Match* in 1938. This was another great success, completely revamping the photo magazine format which had already been around for a few years with *Vu,* founded in 1928, or *Voilà,* launched in 1931 by Gallimard. The trend continued during the Second World War. The German propaganda organ, *Signal,* published in eight languages across occupied Europe, imitated *Match* and published cover photographs of an exceptional quality.

By the end of the 1930s and the Art Deco period, photography was already taking over from illustration. Photographers like Man Ray, Cartier-Bresson or Edward Steichen were competing successfully with the best illustrators, including those on fashion magazines. The economic expansion and social upsets that followed the Second World War affected the whole of the press. Depending on the abilities of the various editors to

adapt or take advantage of the situation, there were winners whose approach seems evident with hindsight and losers who missed the train of modernisation.

Competition from Television

In France, the first publications to lose out after the arrival of television were those who had collaborated during the Occupation. Both *L'Illustration* and *Match* would only reappear in 1949. Many newspapers changed hands, often taken over by former resistance fighters whose popularity in 1944-1945 was inversely proportional to their management abilities.

The reorganisation of press, printing and distribution was undertaken along corporatist union lines with strong state intervention. These structures would put a brake on the necessary development of the sector in France, a much more decisive factor in the retreat of the daily press than the arrival of television.

18

19

After having lost its monopoly on news, the press was now losing its monopoly on the image. Hardest hit were the most recent arrivals: *Paris-Match* only just escaped being closed down; in the United States the unfortunate *Life* did not survive.

The major winners were of course those weeklies which covered television, today accounting for the largest print-runs in the magazine press. *Télé Magazine* was the first French television magazine, appearing in 1955. Other magazines used the television phenomenon to turn themselves into cultural magazines, *Télérama* for example, devoting their covers to the stars of the small screen.

The Resurgence of Magazines

Eventually the magazine press got back into its stride. The *Nouvel Observateur* and *L'Express* heralded the advent of the news magazine in France. Founded in 1950 and 1953 respectively, these two quite austere politico-cultural weeklies with their black and white covers transformed themselves into news magazines and so increased their sales. *L'Express* was radically transformed in 1964, under the editorship of Jean-Jacques Servan-Schreiber, while the *Nouvel Observateur* changed more progressively over the same decade. Similar developments were also under way all over Europe, but covers remained quite traditional. Only a few daring magazines such as *Stern* attempted feats of photomontage like their 1977 cover depicting Chancellor Helmut Schmidt naked. *Stern* reproduced the concept in 2002, this time with Chancellor Schröder in his birthday suit.

As for the women's press, it evolved just as radically as the status of women in society. Before the war, there was a clear separation between the fashion magazines which were luxurious and avant-garde and the traditional periodicals aimed at an audience with more modest means.

In 1937 Prouvost launched *Marie-Claire* with a view to making it 'the poor woman's *Vogue*'. *Marie-Claire* owed its great success to an affordable price, optimistic tone, original layout and cover portraits of women. This winning formula would be reproduced by *Elle* in 1945.

The Rise of Marketing

In the 1960s *Elle* was sold mainly through kiosks. The cover was therefore of supreme importance and the management wondered about its impact on sales. The sociologist Evelyne Sullerot undertook a study involving women readers of *Elle*. She discovered, for example, that brunettes preferred covers depicting brunettes since they identified with them. If these same brunettes suspected their partner of harbouring an appreciation for blondes then they wouldn't buy an issue of *Elle* with a blonde on the cover. Even more unexpected was the discovery that none of the readers consulted appreciated faces that were so tightly framed that the top of the head was cropped or scalped by the top of the page. Sales figures proved the point: issues where the cover showed a woman's face cut off across the top of her head sold fewer copies. All the management had to do was to inform the Art Director of this so that the style could be changed, therefore winning a few thousand extra readers. This anecdote illustrates both the importance of the cover in sales and the efforts made to analyse its impact. In the United States certain tests even went as far as measuring how much the reader sweated as covers were shown to them. A test suitable for *Playboy* perhaps?

The human and financial resources devoted to the creation of covers have increased continuously. The German weekly *Der Spiegel* employs four people for this task alone. The price for sensationalist photos has rocketed, but a successful cover can boost sales by 20 percent.

Nevertheless it is only natural that in a milieu where success has come to be measured exclusively by sales, artistic creativity will suffer. There is now a reluctance to take

risks which might adversely affect sales. The necessity to attract ever greater numbers of readers and, just as importantly, to retain them, has taken precedence over aesthetics and originality. Would a major magazine today entrust a young artist with the creation of a cover as they might have done in the past? Nothing is less sure.

1. *Minotaure.* Couverture, F. Borès, 15th May 1934. Art Director, E. Tériade. **2.** *Harper's Young People.* **3.** *Harper's Weekly.* **4.** *Harper's Weekly.* **5.** *Harper's Young People.* Cover, Culmer Barnes, 8th September 1885. **6.** *Gil Blas.* Cover, Grün, 4th January 1901. **7.** *Münchner Illustrierte.* 3rd May 1952. **8.** *Regards.* September 1952. **9.** *Le petit journal.* 16th September 1906. **10.** *Je sais tout.* November 1929. **11.** *J'ai vu…* 29th December 1917. **12.** *La Baïonnette.* 17th May 1917. **13.** *La Libre Parole.* Cover, Maillotin, 2nd November 1895. **14.** *Life.* 5th June 1939. **15.** *Life.* Cover, Dmitri Kessel, 26th June 1944. Art Director, Worthen Paxton. **16.** *Life.* Cover, Herbert Gehr, 3rd June 1940. Art Directors, Peter Piening and Worthen Paxton. **17.** *Lectures pour tous.* Cover, G. Dutriac, February 1931. **18.** *Le rire.* July 1917. **19.** *V.* Cover, Warner Bros First National, 31st August 1947. **20.** *Elle Japan.*

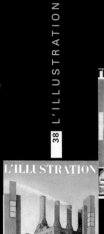

CHAPTER ONE

MAGAZINES

From *Actuel* to *Vu* in alphabetical order, blending news, fashion, politics and eroticism, here is a selection of magazines chosen for the part they have played in the history of graphic design and the development of the image. Discover classic illustrations (*Simplicissimus, The New Yorker*), amazing photography (*National Geographic*), retouched images and photomontages (*Esquire, Interview*), provocative pictures (*Stern, Punch*), seductive spreads (*Lui, Playboy*), unexpected snapshots (*Harper's Bazaar*), exclusive reportage (*Paris Match*), intimate stories (*The Saturday Evening Post*), aggressive aesthetics (*Actuel*), enduring style (*Elle*) and adventurous experimentation (*Vogue*).

The Underground Virus

In 1971 the Freep (Free Press) congress took place at the Baltard Pavilion in Les Halles, the old Paris covered market. In the wake of the events of 1968, the delegates attacked the 'money-grubbing press'. One participant relates: 'Three or four of us got together and decided to produce this thing which was unlike anything else, with splotches and colours, like Wolinski or Crumb, you know. We printed 500 copies. Then we thought we could improve it. Once you start you just don't want to stop.'

Birth of a Counter-Culture

In 1972 there were approximately 150 so-called underground magazines and journals in France, most of them produced in schools, universities or factories. Their names were nothing if not evocative: *Guili-guili* (Tickle Tickle), *L'Égout* (The Sewer), *Le torchon brûle* (The Burning Dishcloth – an angry magazine of the Women's Liberation Movement), *Le Béni-oui-oui* (Yes Man), *Crève Salope* (Die Bitch), *L'Antimerde* (The Antishit), *Le Partageux* (The Distributionist), *Rien* (Nothing), *Vroutsch, Geronanymo, La Cigarette verte* (The Green Cigarette), and *Trépan* (Trepan) were just a few, inspired by the American underground movement. The *Village Voice* led the scene from New York, followed by the East Village *Other,* San Francisco *Oracle,* Los Angeles *Free Press* and the *Fifth Estate* in Detroit. These publications used psychedelic colours and shattered all conventions of layout, often sacrificing legibility for originality. Pop music had a prime role, as well as the personal columns which served to organise new underground grapevines for the exchange of information about subversive, decadent or nefarious activities.

Some of them, vectors of the same counter-culture but more professional, reached a wider public. In France there was the short lived *Tout* (Everything); *Parapluie* (Umbrella); *Zinc; Hara-Kiri* – 'a stupid nasty magazine', banned and then replaced by *Charlie Hebdo* (Weekly Charlie). Above all there was *Actuel.*

In 1968 *Actuel* was a small jazz and pop magazine. In 1971 Jean-François Bizot took the

1

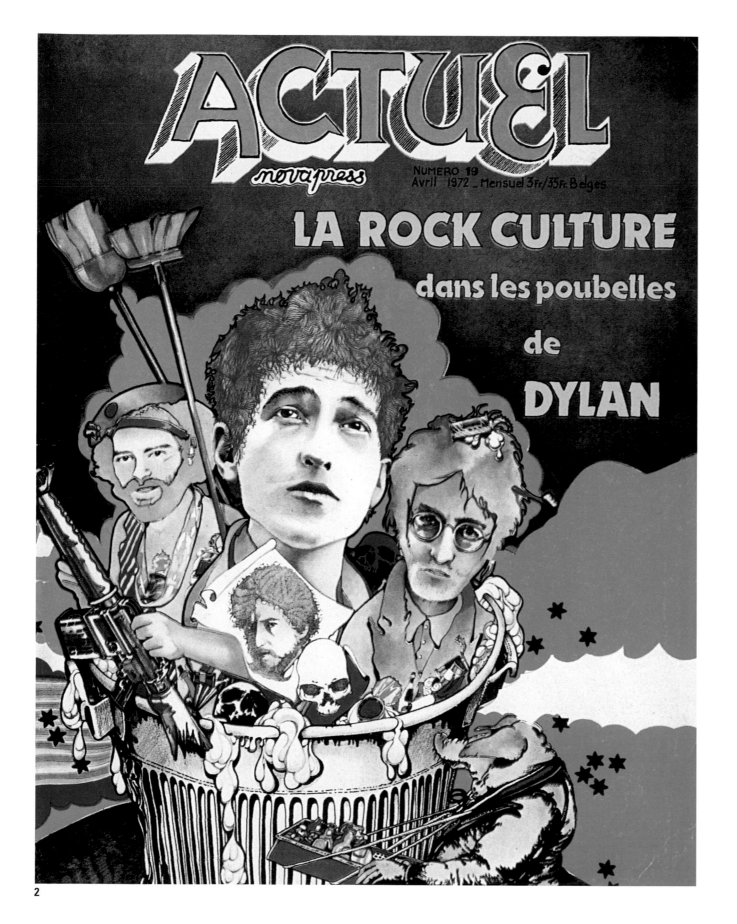

LA ROCK CULTURE

dans les poubelles

de

DYLAN

wheel and changed the formula, turning it into *the* magazine for the hippie generation in France. *Actuel* became a melting pot of exceptional talent and intelligence. These eager, curious and open minds dredged up those titbits of information which appeared nowhere else. The team included, amongst others, Michel-Antoine Burnier, Patrick Rambaud, Bernard Krouchner, Claudine Maugendre, Jean-Pierre Lentin, Léon Mercadet and Patrice Van Eersel. They denounced the formal language of the leftist press, advocating, in the words of Bizot himself, 'subversion through destabilising of traditional family structure using the rock and roll movement as cover'.

The Dangers of Anarchy

The most subversive events received considerable exposure: LSD-fuelled concerts; demonstrations by homosexuals, feminists or ecologists; tales of life in squats or communes; eulogies to nudism; interviews with decadent artists. 'Our watchwords were secrecy, resistance and parasite. The metaphor was of a virus planted in the belly of a vile beast the better to consume it.' The layout provided the terrain for unbridled imagination, while the highly colourful covers emphasised the anarchic, liberated and strongly provocative buzz of the content.

The magazine started to make a slim profit in 1975, yet the editorial team abandoned it out of sheer lassitude. Two annuals appeared nevertheless, before *Actuel* was reborn in a new form in 1979, which survived until 1994. This time, with a nod to the 1980s, the trend was more clean-cut and futuristic, with a larger emphasis on highly photographic reportages from around the world. The formula of the first *Actuel* is irreplaceable, but in the second the pioneering spirit was still there, often imitated but never equalled.

1. Cover by Jérôme de Millo and Jean Chevillard, July to September 1975. **2.** Cover by Benjamin Baltimore, April 1972.

A Right-Wing Anarchist

Despite inventing the slogan 'Mussolini is always right' Leo Longanesi soon fell from grace after a mordant satire on a fascist senator went too far. Such was the paradoxical nature of the founder of *Il Borghese*. Fervently conservative and anti-communist but also deeply independent and anti-conformist, Longanesi was both a brilliant journalist and a talented graphic artist. *Il Borghese* was built in his image. Founded in 1950 this weekly journal aimed to represent the opinion of the Italian Right, independently of any political parties. *Il Borghese* portrayed the microcosm of political and cultural life in Italy with distance and irony. Although the editorial team was tiny (both the cover and the illustrations were created by the editor) and the print-run small, *Il Borghese* had considerable impact on both the public and on politics, as proven by its longevity.

Humour and Scoops

Il Borghese had two fearsome weapons at its disposal. Written in impeccable Italian, articles varied between scathing humour and devastating scoops. In 1954 the magazine revealed the existence of a host of commercial companies belonging to the supposedly anti-capitalist Communist Party. In 1966, a 'leaked' interview resulted in the resignation of the Minister for Foreign Affairs and a governmental crisis. Later on, the weekly would be at the origin of the scandal that brought down the German Chancellor Willy Brandt.

Strong Images

Maintaining the tradition of Longanesi, who died in 1957, *Il Borghese* attached importance to the cover and to witty cartoons and other caricatures that filled its pages. The expression 'a Borghese photograph' has entered the Italian language to describe a photograph which catches its subject in an embarrassing pose or situation. 'Thanks to these photographs', wrote Mario Tedeschi, Longanesi's successor, 'politicians have stopped sticking their fingers up their noses and gorging themselves in restaurants, at least not when there's a photographer hanging about.'

1

2

3

4

5

6

1. 25th April 1968. **2.** 12th September 1968. **3.** 11th April 1968. **4.** 18th April 1968. **5.** 28th March 1968. **6.** 22nd August 1968. **7.** 4th July 1968. **8.** 25th July 1968. **9.** 2nd May 1968. **10.** 1st August 1968. **11.** 20th June 1968.

7

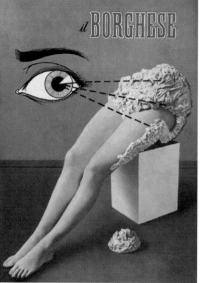

8

9

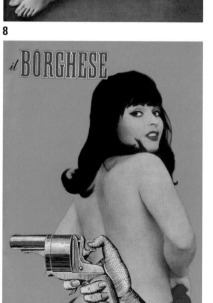

10

11

The New Feminine Look

'We are here to create an appetite.' So said Hélène Gordon Lazareff when explaining the creation – and success – of *Elle* magazine. Hélène Lazareff was the wife of Pierre Lazareff, the most famous journalist in France and veteran of *France Soir,* the newspaper with the largest circulation, as well as *5 Colonnes à la Une,* the first French television news programme. He was certainly a useful backer for what was an original concept in women's magazines.

The start was slow however, for when the first edition appeared in 1945, women's appetites were somewhat limited by rationing. But a new era was opening up and it was in presenting and boosting these new trends that *Elle* magazine became a success. Two themes of particular note which epitomised the magazine were fashion on the cover, and women's liberation inside the magazine itself.

A New Press for a New Woman

With the worldwide success of the New Look by Christian Dior just after the war, Paris reclaimed its position as the capital of fashion. The evolution of female fashion from this era up until today mirrors women's sociological development. The covers of *Elle* reflect these changes.

One major innovation in relation to previous women's magazines was that the content crossed the boundaries traditionally set for women, who were now taken much more seriously. After all, women had finally received the right to vote in France the very year that *Elle* first appeared.

Through her articles Françoise Giroud campaigned for contraception, abortion rights and the improvement of women's place in society generally. *Elle*'s winning formula was soon copied and even equalled by other magazines, but *Elle* remains the benchmark. Unusually, the typography of the title has remained the same from the very first edition.

1

2

3

ELLE
SPÉCIAL

Les résultats de notre Grand Concours (suite)

arts ménagers 1957

N° 583 · 25 FÉVRIER 1957 · 50 FRS · SUISSE : FR. S. · CANADA : 25 CENTS · ITALIE 150 LIRES

4

1. Photo, Jean Lattès, 27th July 1959. **2.** Photo, Dambier, 13th April 1959. Art director, Roger Giret. **3.** Photo, Kazan/Studio Chevalier, 9th January 1956. Art director, Roger Giret. **4.** Photo, Bouillaud/Studio Chevalier-Astorg, 25th February 1957. Art director, Roger Giret.

From Macho to Radical

When *Esquire* was founded in 1933 it aimed to make upper middle-class men aware of male fashion. But so as not to scare readers away by the possibly effeminate nature of a fashion magazine, *Esquire* compensated by including humorous and often slightly misogynistic drawings, short stories by talented young writers, particularly more macho ones like Hemingway or Dashiell Hammet, and intelligent ironic journalism covering current affairs. Its success was immediate and distribution was soon switched from menswear shops to newsagents. In the 1950s *Esquire* became a favourite magazine for students and those who would later be called yuppies.

The Swinging Sixties

Esquire's heyday was definitely the 1960s, when it became more radical, just like its readers. Writers such as Truman Capote or Allen Ginsberg were not so much macho as socially heretical. Their journalism was for the most part satirical. *Esquire* campaigned against the Vietnam War and for liberal values. Under the guiding hand of publicity/design genius George Lois, its covers were of such originality that sales doubled.

The end of the Vietnam War and the return to a consumerist conservatism changed the nature of *Esquire*. There was a noticeable feminisation of the magazine, making it more and more like *Cosmopolitan* or *Elle*. With its machismo attenuated by political correctness *Esquire* no longer had very much to say, although it said it seriously, focussing more on fashion, men's health and sexual issues. Apart from the name, today's *Esquire* has very little in common with that of the 1930s-1960s. But nevertheless, *Esquire* has always stuck to its golden rule: entertain the reader.

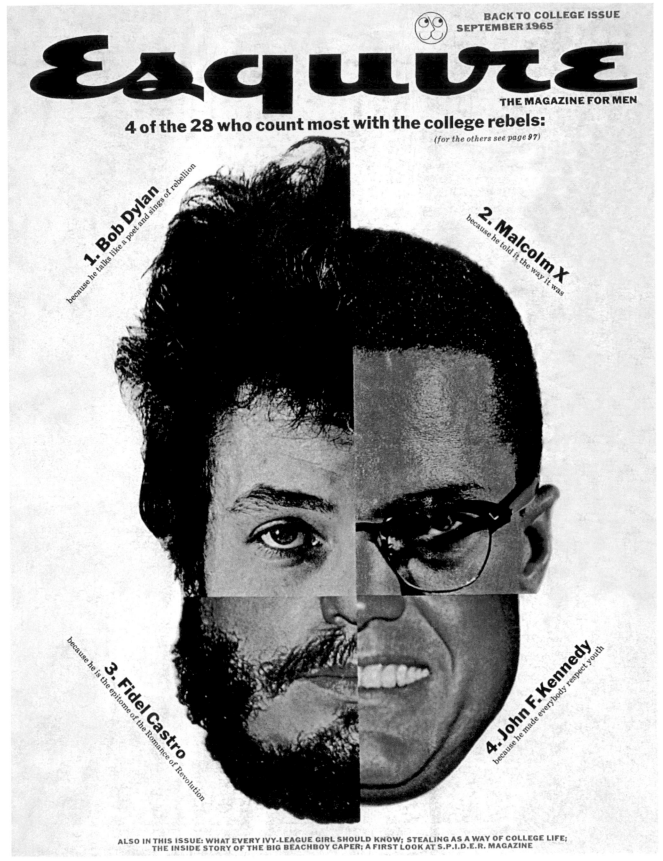

2

3

4

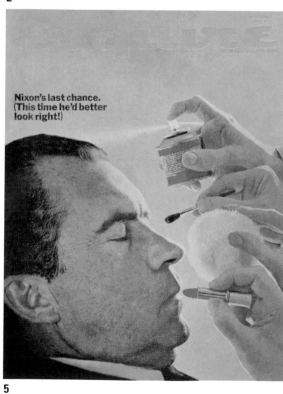

5

6

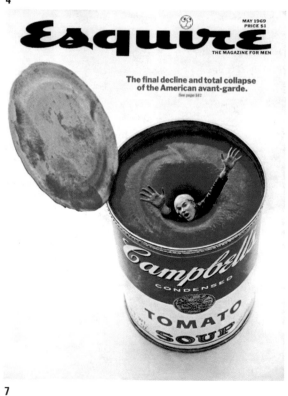

7

1. Photos, Daniel Kramer (Bob Dylan), John Launois (Malcolm X), Mort Tadder (J.F. Kennedy), Wide World (Fidel Castro). Design, George Lois, September 1965. Art Director, Samuel N. Antupit. **2.** Cover, George Lois and Carl Fischer, May 1966. Art Director, Samuel N. Antupit. **3.** Cover, George Lois and Carl Fischer, September 1969. Art Directors, Jean-Paul Goude and Jean Lagarrigue. **4.** Cover, George Lois and Carl Fischer, July 1967. Art Director, Samuel N. Antupit. **5.** May 1968. Art Director, Samuel N. Antupit. **6.** Cover, Jean-Paul Goude and Carl Fischer, April 1969. Art Directors, Jean-Paul Goude and Jean Lagarrigue. **7.** Cover, George Lois and Carl Fischer, May 1969. Art Directors, Jean-Paul Goude and Jean Lagarrigue.

Images of Women for Women

The up-market magazine *Femina* was launched in 1901 by Pierre Laffitte, founder of *La Vie au grand air* (*Life in the Great Outdoors*), *Je sais tout* (I Know Everything), *Musica, Fermes et Châteaux* (Farms and Castles) and in particular the daily *Excelsior* in 1910. His use of photography was revolutionary. *Femina* influenced a whole generation of society women and provided stiff competition to *Le Moniteur de la mode,* well established since 1843 but resolutely devoted to drawings and illustrations. The paper was of the highest quality, as were the photographs, making *Femina* a condensation of the luxury and know-how of the 1900s. The themes tackled were revolutionary too, veering away from the traditional predilections for cookery and embroidery towards fashion, which dominated its covers but was often treated as an issue for debate. One particular issue from 1909 asked 'Is fashion immoral?'

Lower Case Grace

The Art Director was Lucien Vogel, son of a Hachette illustrator, who would become editor of *La Gazette du bon ton* and *Jardin des modes,* founder of *Vu* in 1928 and art director until 1925 of the main rival of *Femina,* the French edition of *Vogue.* His watchwords for the publication were sobriety and elegance. The typography of the title perfectly reflected this aesthetic approach. Although the font itself never changed, its size, colour and position in relation to the rest of the image did. A fine example of this is the discreet counterpoint of the dot on the 'i' for the February 1932 issue (3). But apart from the major use of photography to often surprising effect both inside the magazine and on the cover (1), many illustrators also contributed to the magazine, including René Gruau, André Édouard Marty, Charles Loupot, Umberto Brunelleschi and George Barbier. *Femina* was bought by Hachette in 1916 on the strength of its success.

1

2

3

4

LA SAISON RUSSE A PARIS : CLÉOPATRE

Parmi les attractions de cette saison russe qui a été le véritable évènement de la saison parisienne a figuré le ballet de Cléopâtre, où Mlle Ida Rubinstein mima le rôle de Cléopâtre, avec une grâce de gestes et une étrangeté d'attitudes qui enthousiasmèrent l'assistance charmée. (Voir page 251, les Danseuses russes au Châtelet)

Publications Pierre Lafitte et Cie & 90, Champs-Élysées & Paris

5

1. 1st January 1909. **2.** 15th June 1909. **3.** Cover, C. Haramboure, February 1932. **4.** Cover, P. Mourgue, March 1927. **5.** 1st July 1909.

31

The Aesthetics of Capitalism

Clichés tend to stick. In the collective unconscious capitalists are sad characters who appreciate little except money and huge cigars, disdaining all forms of artistic creativity. The reverse cliché portrays artists as progressive humanists who refuse to be enslaved by the market economy.

Fortune is the most famous economics magazine and the one that best represents the American business world. Yet from its very first issue, in 1930, its founder Henry Luce wished that its covers be undisputably 'the most beautiful'. The idea was to associate the artistic avant-garde with the industrial avant-garde that *Fortune* wished to represent.

The direction was set by the magazine's first art director, Thomas M. Cleland: to present complex technical information in an accessible and aesthetic way. Three European emigré artistic directors succeeded him, each applying the principles of modernism to *Fortune*: Will Burtin (1945-1949), Leo Lionni (1949-1962) and Walter Allner (1962-1974). They called upon the talents of artists such as Herbert Matter, Ladislav Sutnar, Herbert Bayer, Gyorgy Kepes or Lester Beall for the covers and illustrations.

Showcase of the Avant-Garde

This was a period when industrial objects and mechanisms provided the inspiration for numerous artists, from futurists to cubists. Certain works corresponded to themes already covered in the magazine, while some artists received commissions on a particular theme given by the magazine. *Fortune* found itself showcasing the innovative work of artists such as Fernand Léger, George Grosz, Salvador Dalí, Marc Chagall, Max Ernst and Yves Tanguy.

It is interesting to note that certain artists whose political and social values were the opposite of those expounded by *Fortune* nevertheless found themselves contributing to the success of the magazine. *Fortune* did not hesitate to use the talent of Diego Rivera, a marxist painter who hosted Trotsky in Mexico City during his exile.

1

2

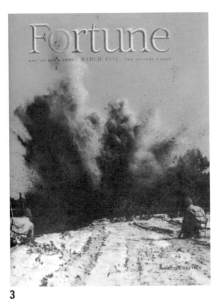

3

4

1. Illustration, Antonio Petruccelli, June 1945. **2.** Illustration, Antonio Petruccelli, September 1933. Art Director, Eleanor Treacy. **3.** Photo, Rudy Arnold, March 1944. Art Director, Peter Pienning. **4.** Illustration, Matthew Leibowitz, December 1947. Art Director, Will Burtin. **5.** Photomontage and painting, Peter Pienning, July 1943. **6.** Illustration, Antonio Petruccelli, September 1937. Art Director, Eleanor Treacy. **7.** Illustration, Robert Crandall, May 1972. Art Director, Walter H. Allner. **8.** Illustration, Allen Saalburg, January 1940. Art Director, Francis E. Brennan. **9.** Illustration, Walter H. Allner, September 1951. Art Director, Leo Leonni.

Overleaf
10. Illustration, Herbert Bayer, August 1940. Art Director, Francis E. Brennan. **11.** Illustration, Edmund Lewandowski, October 1948. Art Director, Will Burtin.

5

6

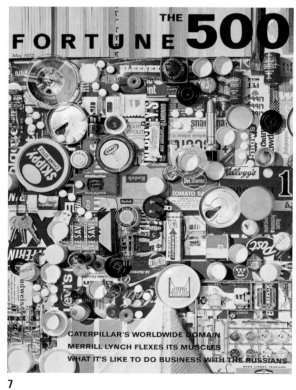

7

8

9

FORTUNE

OCTOBER 1948

...ATION HAS JUST BEGU...

One of the Leaders in Graphic Innovation

*H*arper's Bazar, as it was first spelt, was founded in 1867 in New York by the Harper brothers. It was a women's magazine covering European fashion and it owed its reputation for innovative graphics to collaboration between the greatest layout artists and photographers. During the Belle Époque (1890-1914) special attention was paid to covers since they represented Parisian haute couture, particularly the Worth fashion house. In 1913 William Randolph Hearst, the American press magnate who would be immortalised in Orson Welles's film *Citizen Kane,* bought *Harper's Bazar* with the intention of making it the rival of *Vogue.* Not content with adding an additional, anglicising 'a' to the title, Hearst invested heavily in the magazine with profits from his press group.

A Rival to *Vogue*

The editorial style of the magazine was both amusing and aristocratic. From 1924 to 1937 (when the magazine was sold a second time), the fashion illustrations and covers were designed exclusively by Erté, former assistant of the couturier Poiret. His characteristic silhouettes became a key element of the magazine. Using the tried and tested methods that had enabled him to build his empire, Hearst poached the best photographers from *Vogue* and also hired Carmel Snow, who became the editor of *Harper's Bazaar.* He modernised the magazine by using writers such as Jean Cocteau, who also provided drawings, and top photographers like Man Ray.

Snow invited Alexey Brodovitch, hitherto teaching a course in advertising, to work as art director. He would remain at the magazine for 25 years, from 1934 to 1958, redefining the role of art director (3, 4, 5) and making challenging inroads into both typography and fashion photography. He was succeeded by Henry Wolf, who had been art director of Esquire since 1952. Wolf attracted the talents of renowned artists such as Ben Sahn or Richard Lindner, and himself designed some highly original covers for *Harper's Bazaar*

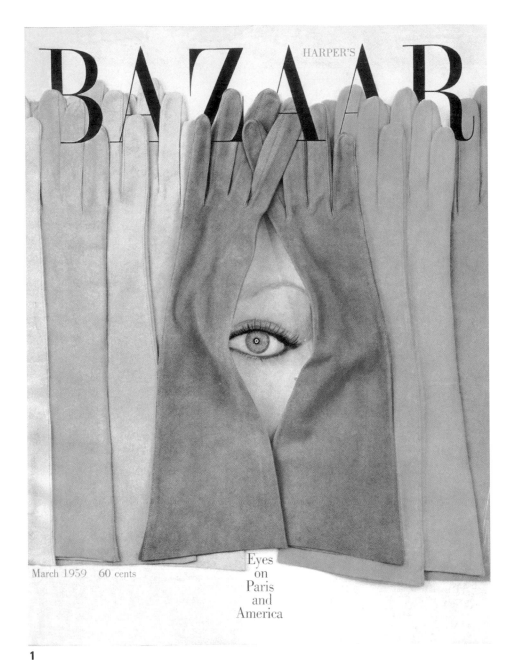

1

2

1. Photo, Ben Rose, March 1959. Art Director, Henry Wolf. **2.** Photo, Moore, May 1964. Art Directors, Ruth Ansel and Bea Feitler. **3.** Photo, Richard Avedon, February 1952. Art Directors, Alexey Brodovitch and Jack Dunbar. **4.** November 1935. **5.** Photo, Richard Avedon, September 1955. Art Directors, Alexey Brodovitch and Adrian Johns.

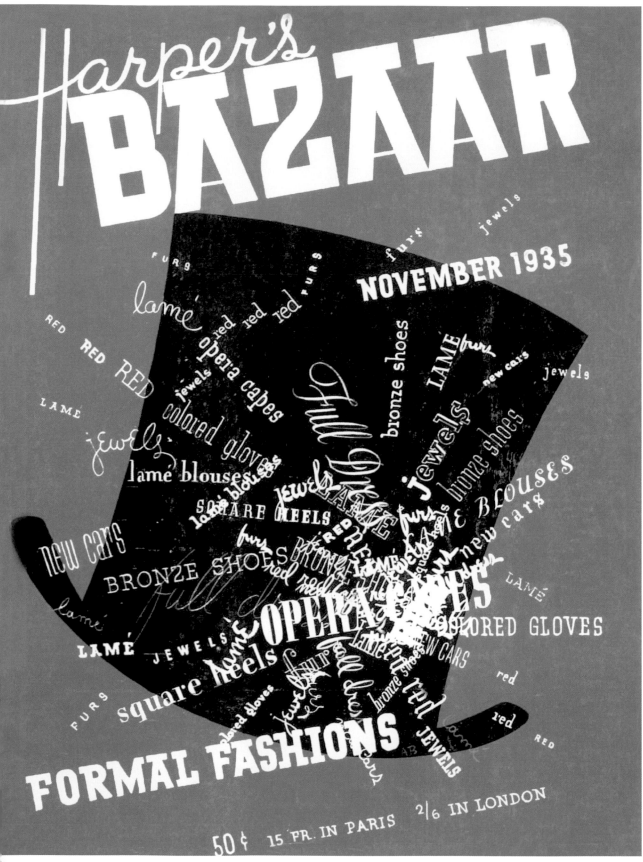

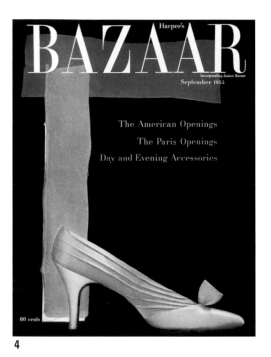

4

which were sharp yet subtle photomontages using very precise studio photographs (1).

Harper's Bizarre

During this period the magazine overturned many stylistic conventions, both photographic and typographic. Original layouts were the order of the day, from title lettering partially masked by an image (1) or impertinently covering the face of a model (2), to changing the font of the title (3). *Harper's Bazaar* is still one of the most important fashion magazines in the United States, although it has not been graced with any such spectacular renewal as that which it underwent in the golden years of the 1930s-1960s. Today it targets middle-aged women, while the sophistication and aesthetic quality of the French and Italian editions surpass that of their American parent.

3

A Century of Images

Founded in Paris in 1843 following the model of the British *Illustrated London News, L'Illustration,* the 'universal journal' as it liked to call itself, had a particularly long life, appearing for 101 years. From its inception, the quality of its articles and pictures, as well as its use of the latest technological innovations, made it the most prestigious magazine of the era. In 1891, it was the first journal to publish snapshots. As its name indicates it had a particular focus on images, firstly drawings and then photographs, but always with great care taken regarding their aesthetic qualities.

The Journal of the Elite

A weekly news magazine, *L'Illustration* also had a literary section written by eminent critics which was read most attentively. In general it called upon the talents of reputed journalists who would guarantee its continued prestige. For the bourgeois intellectual elite it was very much the done thing to subscribe to *L'Illustration,* even (or perhaps because) it was an expensive magazine, compared with its cheaper imitators such as *Le Petit Journal illustré, La France illustrée* or *L'Illustré national.* From a print run of 18,000 in 1866 (compared with 33,000 for *Le Monde Illustré,* its closest rival), it reached 200,000 in 1939, with peaks of 400,000 for certain special issues published during the First World War. Its success was such that a new printing works had to be built, one of the most modern in Europe, at Bobigny, in the Paris suburbs. These facilities were intended to serve *L'Illustration* and its sister publications comprising *La Petite Illustration,* which was more literary, containing plays and short stories, and *Plaisir de France,* a luxury monthly launched by the same group in 1934. Faithful to republican ideals until the end of the 19th century, *L'Illustration* shifted clearly to the right after the First World War. In 1936 it expressed its hostility to the coalition, then to the government of the Popular Front. It ceased publication after the Liberation of France, banned, by the decree of 6th May 1944, like all the other periodicals that had continued to appear under the Occupation.

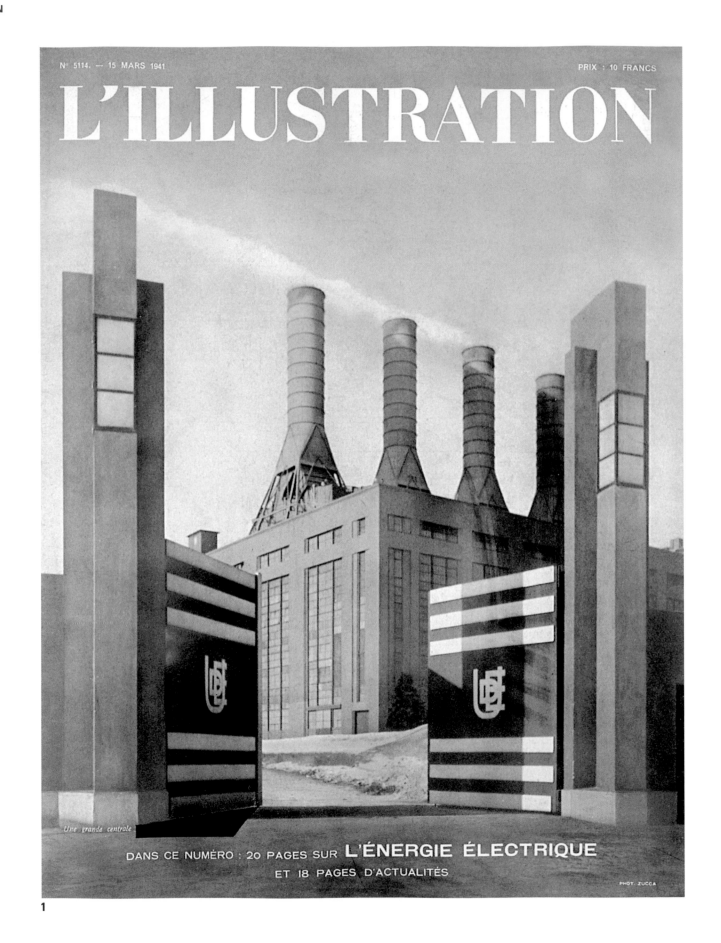

Nᵒ 5114. — 15 MARS 1941   PRIX : 10 FRANCS

L'ILLUSTRATION

Une grande centrale

DANS CE NUMÉRO : 20 PAGES SUR **L'ÉNERGIE ÉLECTRIQUE**
ET 18 PAGES D'ACTUALITÉS

PHOT. ZUCCA

1

L'ILLUSTRATION
EXPOSITION
1937

14 AOUT 1937
PRIX 10 FRANCS

LES MUSÉES D'ART MODERNE
Dondel, Aubert, Viard, et Dastugue, architectes

2

1. Illustration, Zucca, 31st March 1941. 2. 14th August 1937. Art Director, Jacques Baschet.

Andy Warhol's Baby

'Why start a magazine? So we could get free tickets to all the premieres' It was with these words that Andy Warhol founded *Interview* in 1969. He had arrived in New York twenty years before, aged 21, to launch his career as an illustrator for magazines such as *Vogue, Harper's Bazaar* and *The New Yorker.* Crazy about magazines, it was logical that he should found his own. He had already created his famous screen prints of Campbell's Soup Cans, Coca-Cola bottles and portraits of Marilyn Monroe. But the press was unexplored territory. His fascination with the world of Hollywood and pop culture assured the magazine's success.

Initially covering the cinema, it soon expanded to include stars of all kinds, integrating fashion, music, art and the multiple facets of New York nightlife, all subjected to Warhol's jaunty treatment.

The choice of a large format (10¹/² x 16 inches) made possible a spectacular layout featuring cover portraits of showbiz personalities, all given the Warhol touch. Warhol commissioned young artists such as Bruce Weber, Steven Meisel or Herb Ritts, all of whom would become great photographers in their own right. The aim was to showcase rising talent and depict established stars from a different angle.

Pell-Mell

Inside, the only layout rule seemed to be the lack of one. Everything was mixed together in no apparent order, from articles to adverts to news items concerning artistic events that rocked the Big Apple. The house speciality, as its name indicated, was the interview, but with a twist. Stars were interviewed by other stars. The resulting articles are deliciously subjective, since the interviewer's viewpoint is often as revealing as the content.

The magazine's success grew steadily. In 1987, the year of Warhol's death, its print run was 170,000. It is still going strong.

JOHNNY DEPP **PLUS ALL-MALE REVUE**

APRIL $ 2.50 U.K. £ 2.30

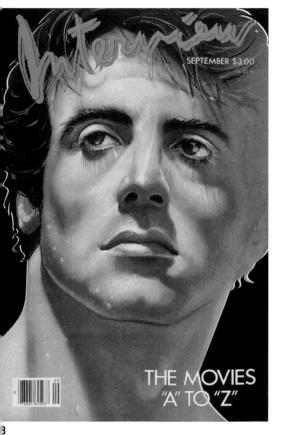

1. April 1990. Art Director, Fabien Baron. 2. April 1986. Art Director, Marc Balet. 3. September 1985. Art Director, Marc Balet. 4. February 1981. Art Director, Marc Balet.

Overleaf
5. Poster, Alexander Rodchenko, July 1988. Art Director, Angelo Savaïdes. 6. Photo, Francesco Scavullo, May 1973. Art Director, Glenn O'Brien. 7. January 1988. Art Director, Henry Connel.

5

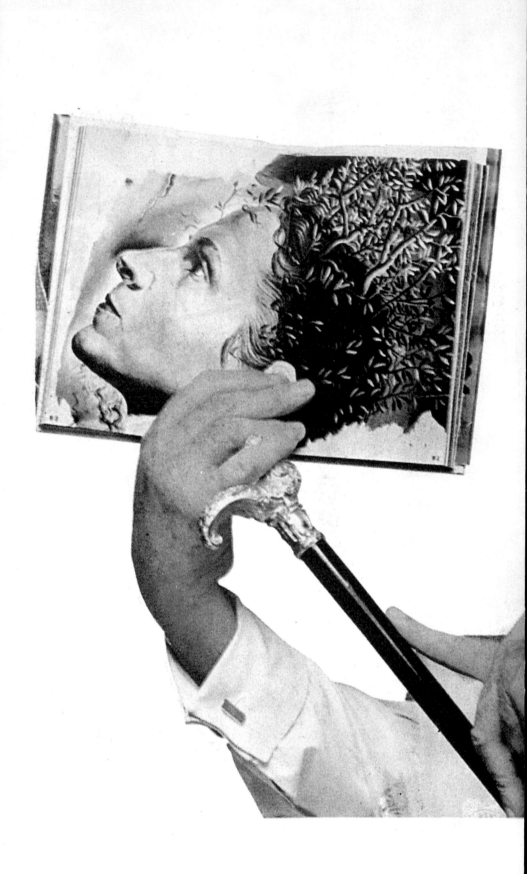

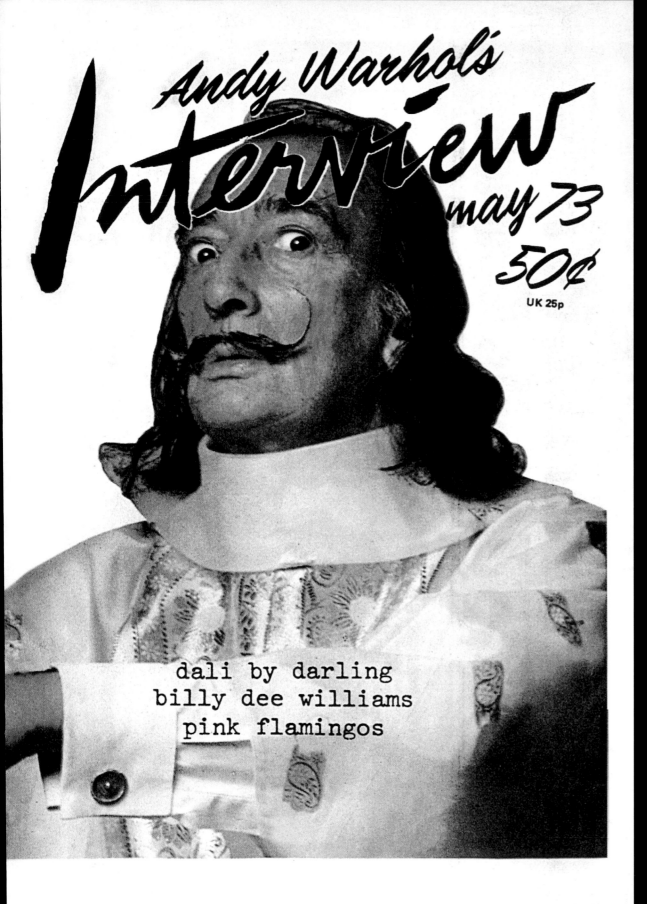

dali by darling
billy dee williams
pink flamingos

TRACEY ULLMAN

Emblematic of Post-War Germany

Founded in 1946, *Kristall* – which promised an 'exceptional magazine to inform and entertain' – belongs to the ephemeral galaxy of German illustrated periodicals born after the war. One year before *Kristall,* the famous *Heute* inspired by *Life* (itself inspired by the *Berliner Illustrierte* of the 1920s) had been founded. *Der Stern, Quick* and the *Frankfurter Illustrierte* all appeared in 1948, followed two years later by the *Münchner Illustrierte* and the *Bunte Illustrierte.* Owned by Hammerich & Lesser in Hamburg, the journal was initially called *Nordwestdeutsche Hefte,* but Ivar Lissner, the editor, was looking for a catchier title. The journal would appear as *Kristall* for the first time in the middle of 1948. After 1949 the German press was no longer dependent upon the authorisation for publication granted by the provisional American administration. From then on the number of different magazines present on the newsstands increased considerably; by the start of the 1950s more than twenty titles were available to the public, with *Quick* and *Neuer Illustrierte* heading sales. *Kristall* would also benefit from this public enthusiasm for the press. Although Ivar Lissner was replaced as editor in 1953 by Paul Hünehnenfeld, the editorial line remained the same. *Kristall* offered its readers high quality photographic reportages. Some of the greatest names in photojournalism worked for the magazine, including Robert Lebeck, Rosemarie Clausen or Jochen Blume. Moreover, the texts which took up a large part of the magazine, whether fiction or current affairs, were written by renowned German authors such as Heinz Lipman, a journalist and man of the theatre, whose novel *Rasputin* would be published by the magazine as a serial.

The World of Axel Springer

In 1958 the title changed hands. Axel Springer bought *Kristall* and started to build his empire with the newspapers *Hamburger Abendblatt, Die Welt, Welt am Sonntag,* and the magazines *Das Neue Blatt* and *Hör zu.* The title that would soon make his fortune, *Bild,* appeared in 1952. *Kristall* certainly did not attract the same readership as *Bild,* but times had

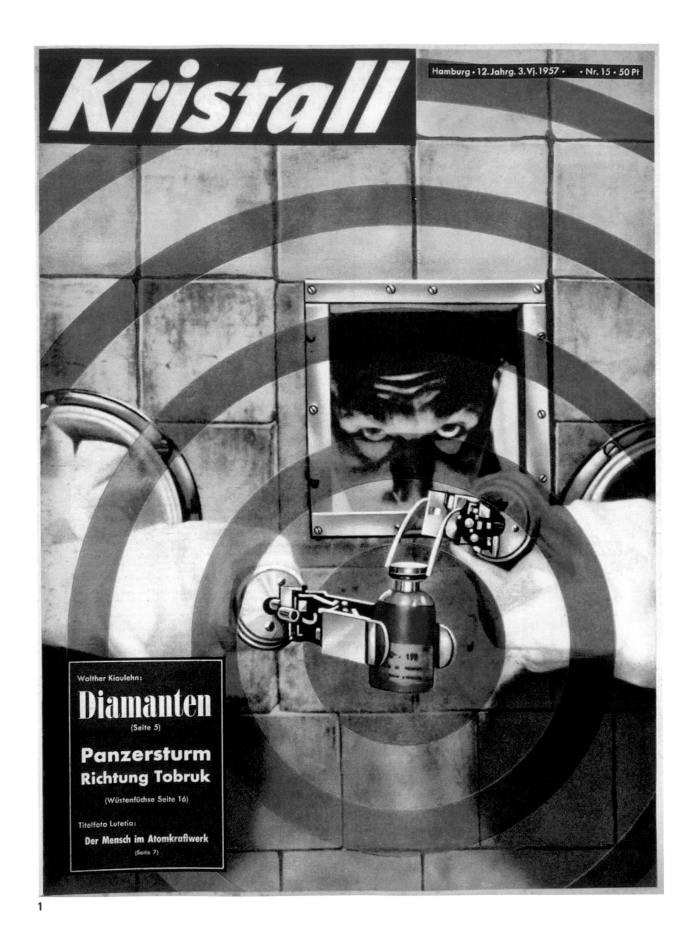

1

3

THE SAND WITCH

4

LONG DISTANCE MAKES THE HEART GROW FONDER

5

1776 - RETOUCHING AN OLD MASTERPIECE - 1915

6

7

technique, where part of a figure was blended into the background colour (3). Just as the Gibson Girl marked the turn of the century, so her younger sister, the Fadeaway Girl, became the fantasised feminine image of the 1910s-1920s, an evanescent woman placed in everyday settings whose intimate yet modest poses seemed to have been captured without her realising. This technique was well suited to monochrome printing, enabling *Life* to make savings and yet produce an elegant cover, when other magazines had already adopted the more expensive colour process. But when *Life* finally made the switch to colour in 1908, it was still the Fadeaway Girl who inaugurated it.

New *Life*

Life was bought in 1935 by Henry Luce, the editor of *Time.* In November 1936 it became the magazine that we all know, with its new format revolutionising the traditional press. The text now took second place to the spectacular photographic reportages for which the magazine paid handsomely. Sales of 250,000 copies were expected. In just a few months they were printing over a million. The Golden Age of photojournalism had arrived.

1. Illustration, James Montgomery Flagg, 23rd March 1905. **2.** Illustration, R. B. Robinson, 2nd September 1909. **3.** Illustration, C. Coles Phillips, 13th June 1909. **4.** Illustration, C. Coles Phillips, 22nd July 1909. **5.** Illustration, C. Coles Phillips, 9th February 1911. **6.** Illustration, Paul Stahr, 1st July 1915. **7.** 2nd January 1908.

A Picture Book

Founded in October 1888 by G. G Hubbard, the goal of The National Geographic Society was the 'increase and diffusion of geographical knowledge'. To assist in accomplishing this mission, the Society produced its own eponymous journal. The first issue was presented as a scientific brochure, with a forbidding terracotta coloured cover. Under the direction of Edwin Grosvenor, this unattractive technical journal would be transformed into a popular publication with a glossy cover bursting with colour. From February 1910 a yellow border framed a grey band set with four globes. A pioneer of colour photography, the *National Geographic* was rewarded by the Photographic Society of America in 1953. Under the editorship of Melville Grosvenor, the magazine was modernised. The July 1959 issue, bearing the American flag, marked the permanent adoption of the cover photograph. Five months after this star spangled cover *The National Geographic Magazine* became *Geographic Magazine* and finally, in March 1960, *National Geographic.*

The World at Its Best?

Though creative in style, the *National Geographic* has not always been audacious in content. Indeed it has often been accused of depicting 'a smiling, pleasant world, free from political intrigue, commercial interest, disease and sin' (*Newsweek,* 11th November 1963). Melville Grosvenor answered these criticisms without mincing his words: 'Since the world contains so many marvels, why the

1. July 1956. **2.** October 1959. Art Director, Andrew Poggenpohl. **3.** Cover, Helen and Frank Schreider, October 1960. Art Director, Andrew Poggenpohl. **4.** Photo, Nasa. Illustration, Robet C. Magis, June 1962. Art Director, Andrew Poggenpohl. **5.** Cover, Howard Sochurek, April 1968. Art Director, Howard E. Paine. **6.** Cover, Naresh and Rajesh Bedi, September 1970. **7.** Cover, Loren McIntyre, October 1972. Art Director, Andrew Poggenpohl. **8.** Cover, Robert W. Madden, March 1975. Art Director, Howard E. Paine. **9.** Cover, Loren McIntyre, November 1977. Art Director, Howard E. Paine. **10.** Cover, Howard Nelson, April 1978. Art Director, Howard E. Paine. **11.** Cover, Bruce Dale, March 1980. Art Director, Howard E. Paine. **12.** Cover, Rod Brindamour, June 1980. Art Director, Howard E. Paine.

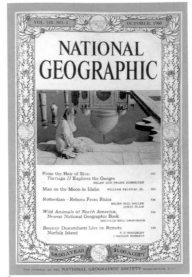
1

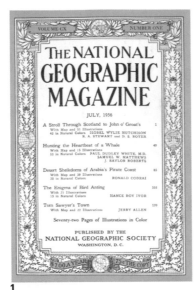
2

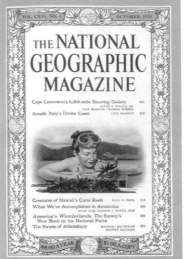
3

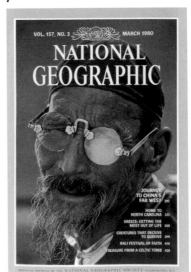
4

5

6

7

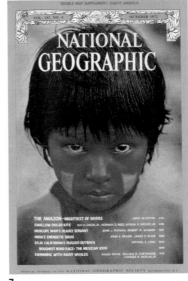
8

9

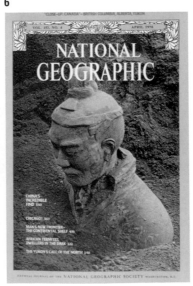
10

11

12

14

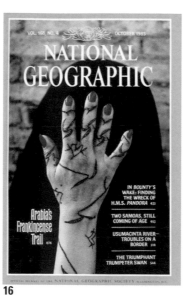
16

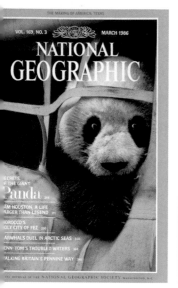

18

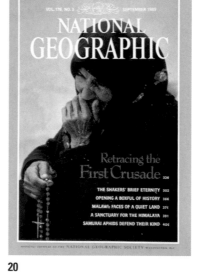
20

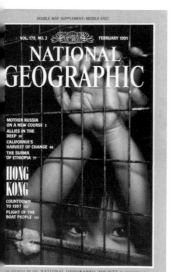

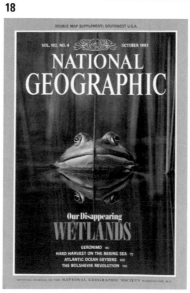
22

hell dwell on the sordid?' His ten-year tenure as editor was certainly a success. From 2,178,040 subscribers in 1957, the number had risen to 5,607,457 in 1967.

From Pole to Pole

Nevertheless, the *National Geographic* did start to devote space to some of the harsher realities of the world – the Vietnam War, the assassinations of Robert F. Kennedy and Martin Luther King, the Six Day War, the Soviet invasion of Czechoslovakia and the famine in Biafra. Although the magazine prudently maintained its objectivity, it no longer ignored such subjects. The December 1970 reportage entitled 'Our Ecological Crisis' marked a turning point towards a more campaigning form of journalism. Despite the reticence of the Society's board of directors, Gilbert Grosvenor, appointed editor in 1970, introduced such sensitive subjects as Cuba under Castro, life in Harlem and separatism in Quebec. The reportage 'South Africa's Lonely Ordeal', published in June 1977, symbolised the new realism that Gilbert Grosvenor wished to promote.

His successor, Bill Garrett, continued in the same direction. The journal continued to publish its classic photographs of space (Voyager I), nature (the mountain gorillas of Dian Fossey) and adventure (the first crossing of the Pacific), but also politically provocative photographs, covering subjects such as the killing fields of Cambodia, AIDS, or drugs in Spanish Harlem. In 1984 the quality of the journal earned it the Prize of Excellence, one of the most prestigious awards in journalism. In the 1990s, photographers were encouraged to affirm their own vision of the world, therefore reinforcing the artistic aspect of their photographs. Often unusual, always striking, these photographs are the true mark of the *National Geographic* which, a century after its creation, has a circulation of more than 10 million copies in 160 countries.

13. Cover, Steve Wall, September 1981. Art Director, Howard E. Paine. **14.** Cover, Des and Jen Bartlett, June 1982. Art Director, Howard E. Paine. **15.** Cover, Steve McCurry, December 1984. Art Director, Howard E. Paine. **16.** Cover, Lynn Abercrombie, October 1985. Art Director, Howard E. Paine. **17.** Cover, George B.Schaller, March 1986. Art Director, Howard E. Paine. **18.** Cover, Chris Johns, July 1987. Art Director, Howard E. Paine. **19.** Cover, Bruno Barbey, July 1988. Art Director, Howard E. Paine. **20.** Cover, Peter Essick, September 1989. Art Director, Howard E. Paine. **21.** Cover, Jodi Cobb, February 1991. Art Director, Howard E. Paine. **22.** Cover, Mark Wilson, October 1992. Art Director, Allen Carroll.

An Illustrated Magazine for the Big Apple

The New Yorker was the creation of one man, Harold Ross. An admirer of European satirical magazines such as *Simplicissimus* in Germany or *Punch* in London, he was sure that there was room in the American market for a weekly purveyor of fine wit in tune with the cultural beat and mindset of New York, his adopted home. Convinced that the inhabitants of the Big Apple were in a class of their own, he chose to address a select, demanding and moneyed readership who deserved a journal that spoke their language and was neatly in step with their lives.

Bull's-Eye

Ross was right. Not only was *The New Yorker* a great success with the New York intelligentsia, but it also attracted urbanites elsewhere who dreamed of belonging to the same élite. For Ross was selling not only a magazine but a lifestyle that bore the mark of the city to beat all cities. In the 1930s, with the Great Depression in full swing and the whiff of war already in the air, *The New Yorker* appeared as a haven of humour and refinement, treating even the most serious issues through caricature and satire instead of weighty rhetoric. A new concept was born. Its covers were always painted or drawn with a quirky elegance that somehow avoided the vagaries of fashion.

But although the magazine's readership was considered to be quite respectable, Ross did not take himself too seriously, lauding its 'eccentric editorial leader, disorganized and unreliable staff, and unexpected success rewarding creative chaos in the absence of an editorial plan.' It covered everything from sporting news to portraits of personalities, political satire, a guide to the essential cultural events, film, theatre, art and restaurant reviews and practical subjects of interest to its readers' tastes – fashion, real estate and travel, as

1. Illustration, Bob Knox, 15th July 1991. 2. Illustration, "Family values" by Art Spiegelman, 22nd April 1996. 3. Illustration, "Under the Cloud" by Lorenzo Mattotti, 31st July 1995. 4. Illustration, "On the Beach" by R. Sikoryak, 26th January 1998.

1

2

3

4

5

6

10

12

13

7

well as a guest column entitled 'Why I Like New York'. Despite differing styles and opinions the answer to this question was essentially always the same: it's dirty, crowded and unhealthy but I couldn't imagine living anywhere else!

Harold Ross retained editorial control until his death in 1951. William Shawn succeeded him until 1987, followed by Robert Gottlieb, Tina Brown and now David Remnick. Each has left their indelible mark on the magazine.

The New Yorker has never pretended to be representative of America but rather reflects the vision and values of a relatively small élite. So how can one explain its nationwide success? Firstly because of the fascination that America's cultural capital holds, and secondly because the magazine was able to create a new kind of witty humour otherwise unknown in the United States.

8

9

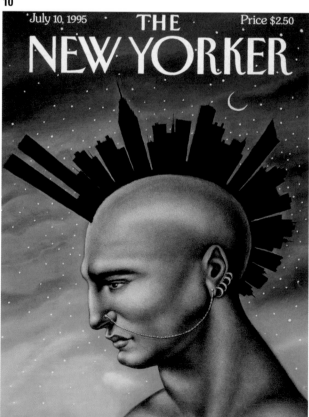

11

5. Illustration, "Irreconcilable Differences" by Bruce Eric Kaplan, 13th November 2000. 6. Illustration, "The Pope in the City" by Barry Blitt, 9th October 1995. 7. Illustration, "Ninety-five Fools" by Richard Mc Guire, 3rd April 1995. 8. Illustration, "The Writing Life" by Owen Smith, 25th December 1995 to 1st January 1996. 9. Illustration, "Where the Heart Is" by Ana Juan, 16th October 1995. 10. Illustration, Iriksen, 29th May 1995. 11. Illustration, "Mohawk Manhattan" by Anita Kunz, 10th July 1995. 12. Illustration, Gürbüz Dogan Eksioglu, 18th January 1993. 13. Illustration, "Upwardly Mobile" by Eric Drooker, 30th September 1996.

Literature and Politics

The North American Review is a real institution in the United States, as much for its quality as its longevity. Founded in 1815, it is probably one of the oldest journals in the world. It is published by the University of Northern Iowa, which provides for it financially and establishes its editorial guidelines, concentrating on literary texts, short stories, poems and reviews, as well as essays on art, politics and social problems.

Founded after the War of 1812 against the British, the first issues of the journal were essentially political in content. This was an era when pro and anti-British partisans confronted each other in opposing newspapers and journals. The North American Review was created by the Anthology Club of Boston with the aim of propagating British culture and influence in America, while still pursuing the noble aims of arousing interest in the arts and literature in its fellow citizens. Despite a limited circulation of 3,000 copies, it won over a progressive readership and wielded considerable political, social and financial influence.

The life of The North American Review during its first few decades was a quiet one. The philosopher Emerson even wrote that one could hear 'the snoring of the muses' in its pages. Around 1850 the journal got rather livelier, with writers like James Russell Lowell, Charles Eliot Norton or Henry Adams taking turns in the editor's chair.

The American Civil War (1861-1865) completely changed the role of the press in the United States. Out of this fratricidal war was born a new industrial and capitalist America. This transformation of American society resulted in the appearance of a new form of journalism that wielded more influence on the social and political life of America.

The number of periodicals increased, with all nature of subjects tackled. Their various styles took shape, while the audacity and seriousness of their investigations heralded the arrival of today's 'fourth estate'. The North American Review, as well as The New Harper's Monthly Magazine, The Nation and The Atlantic Monthly gave a real direction to

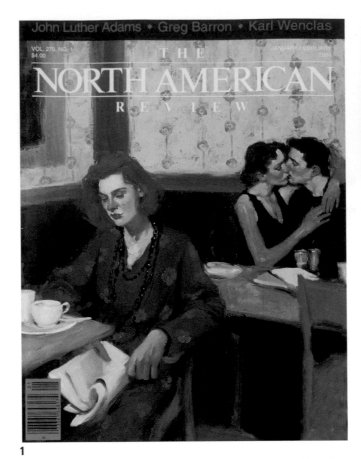

1

2

3

4

5

6

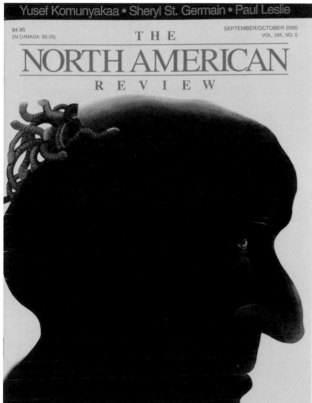

7

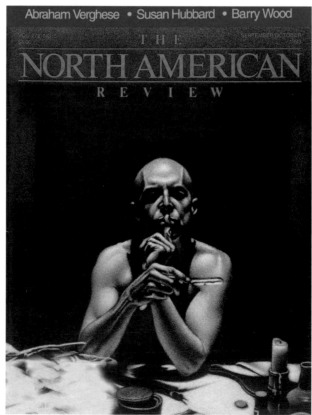

8

debate, while continuing to direct American literary life.

An Avant-Garde Journal

The glory days of *The North American Review* came at the end of the 1870s, when it was bought by Allen Thorndike Rice. He moved the journal's head office from Boston to New York and attracted the major writers of the period. Very soon the journal was publishing distinguished articles that are still revered today, including the thoughts of Whitman on the future of poetry, Mark Twain's implacable critique of missionaries, entitled 'To the Person Sitting in Darkness', or the essay 'Wealth' by the rich industrial and philanthropist Andrew Carnegie, in which he stated that private fortunes should serve the general good. Henry James and Joseph Conrad also wrote serials for it. *The North American Review*, whose declared anglophilic slant became less and less palpable as the century wore on, set itself to denouncing the abusive policies of major trusts, political corruption and the obscure workings of political parties.

But the emergence of muckraking newspapers at the start of the 20th century heralded the slow decline of *The North American Review*, which had always rejected the sensationalist aspects of journalism in favour of serious debate. The Second World War dealt it a fatal blow and it ceased publication in 1940. It was reborn in 1964, thanks to Robert Dana of Cornell College, Iowa, into whose premises the newspaper moved in 1968.

Over the last twenty years *The North American Review* has distinguished itself by winning a number of literary prizes, including for Best American Short Story, Best American Essay, Best American Sports Writing and Best American Travel Writing.

1. Oil, "The Corner Table", Skip Liepke. January-February 1994. **2.** Cover, Gary Kelley. May-June 1993. **3.** Cover, Robert M. Cunningham. July-August 1996. **4.** March-April 2001. **5.** Cover, Étienne Delessert. March-April 1993. **6.** Cover, Robert Crawford. September-October 1999. **7.** Cover, Étienne Delessert. September-October 2000. **8.** Cover, Blair Benz. September-October 1993.

Hard-Hitting Pictorials

In 1938 Jean Prouvost was a magnate of the French press. The jewel in his empire was *Paris-Soir*, edited by Pierre Lazareff. Apart from its excellent editorial management, the success of *Paris-Soir* was due to the images it published, taking up 50% of the front page, a record in the daily French press.

In the 1920s and 1930s all the conditions that would allow photojournalism to flourish were brought together. The aeroplane had considerably reduced travel time for reporters to reach their story, while the belinograph, the precursor of the fax machine, enabled photographs to be sent over telephone lines. These technical advances fed the public's increasing enthusiasm for a daily dose of images of places and people they had only ever heard about but never seen. At the same time, the place of writing was shifting from pure information to opinion, as the image was transformed, rightly or wrongly, into evidence backing the journalist's view.

Match, the French *Life*

In 1936, the revamped *Life* was launched with great success. It brought the best photographers, writers and journalists together. Always on the lookout for fresh opportunities, Jean Prouvost was intent on copying its success. In 1938 he bought the sporting weekly *Match* and reworked it following the *Life* model. It was an astounding success. Circulation rose from 80,000 to 1.4 million in less than two years, before the war stopped publication. After the Liberation, the reappearance of *Match* was delayed by Prouvost's legal entanglements (he had briefly participated in Pétain's first government). In 1949 *Match* was re-launched as *Paris Match,* with a brilliant team including Roger Thérond, Raymond Cartier and many others. It was another great success, thanks to dramatic events that included the coronation of Elizabeth II and the battle of Diên Biên Phu. This was the golden age of the magazine; in 1958 *Paris Match* had a print-run of 1.8 million copies .

Decline set in with the advent of television. An ageing Jean Prouvost was unable to work his magic and set a new course, despite

1

2

3

1. Photo, Gamma. Illustration, after a poster by Picasso, 3rd November 1973.
2. Photo, Jacques Langevin/Sygma, 15th June 1989. 3. Photo, Franz Goess, 31st August 1968. 4. Photo, Patrick Robert/Sygma, 18th April 1991. Art Director, Guy

Trillat. 5. Photo, Lennart Nilsson/Time Life © 1965, 12th February 1966. Art Director, Jacques Bourgeas.

PARIS MATCH

KURDES L'HORREUR

C'est l'exode de tout un peuple, à travers le froid, la faim, le désespoir.

DES PHOTOS COMMENTEES POUR NOUS PAR DANIELLE MITTERRAND

CHRISTINE VILLEMIN
La fin de son calvaire : deux témoins retrouvent la mémoire !

SCANDALE KENNEDY
Nuit agitée à Palm Beach, en Floride. Victime de viol dans la maison de Ted, une femme accuse...

LE NOUVEAU NOAH
Il sera chanteur et s'occupera de ses enfants.

«Mon Dieu! Le regard de cet enfant... Il accuse le monde entier.» Danielle Mitterrand, présidente de France Libertés, réagit face à la tragédie kurde. Elle ajoute, bouleversée : «Qui ne pense pas à son propre enfant en voyant cette image?»

journalists' warnings of the impending slump that would hit the weekly magazine market. *Life* ceased publication in 1976, paradoxically just after the Vietnam War had seen a complete renewal of photojournalism. There was still a place for *Paris Match* as long as it adapted to the new realities of the market.

In 1976 Daniel Filipacchi bought *Paris Match* from Prouvost. The magazine had lost two thirds of its readership. Roger Thérond took over as editor, carving out a niche for the weekly somewhere between television and the rest of the press, focussing on detailed articles instead of fresh news; banal and hastily printed snapshots were replaced by stunning colour photographs that were selected from thousands for their unique aesthetic value or significance. Sales started to rise again, levelling off at around a million copies. Today *Paris Match* remains an institution and one of the premier French news magazines.

PARIS MATCH N° 879 12 FEVRIER 1966 / 1.20 F

En couleurs des documents photographiques sans précédent : comment l'enfant grandit dans le sein de sa mère.

LA VIE AVANT LA NAISSANCE

5

A pioneer of Photojournalism

Picture Post appeared for the first time in 1938. It was financed by Edward George Hulton, son of the press magnate Edward Hulton. It was a stunning success, and in just four months its circulation reached 1,350,000 copies a week. Though a very British magazine, most of its editorial team were not. Stefan Lorant, the editor, was a Hungarian who had left his country after the First World War, while the two photography editors, Hans Baumann (credited as Felix H. Man) and Kurt Hubschmann (credited as K. Hutton) came straight from Germany, where they had already been working in the press.

Campaigning

When Lorant emigrated to the United States in 1940, Tom Hopkinson took over the editorship. He turned the magazine into a virulently anti-Nazi tool, vigorously denouncing the persecution of the Jews. On the 26th of November 1938, he had been behind a series of photographs entitled *Return to the Middle Ages,* where he contrasted ferocious portraits of

1

2

3

4

5

1. 14th September 1946. 2. 1st June 1940. 3. 14th October 1939. 4. 27th May 1939. 5. 20th June 1942. 6. 2nd August 1947.

Overleaf
7. 9th September 1939. 8. 14th September 1940.

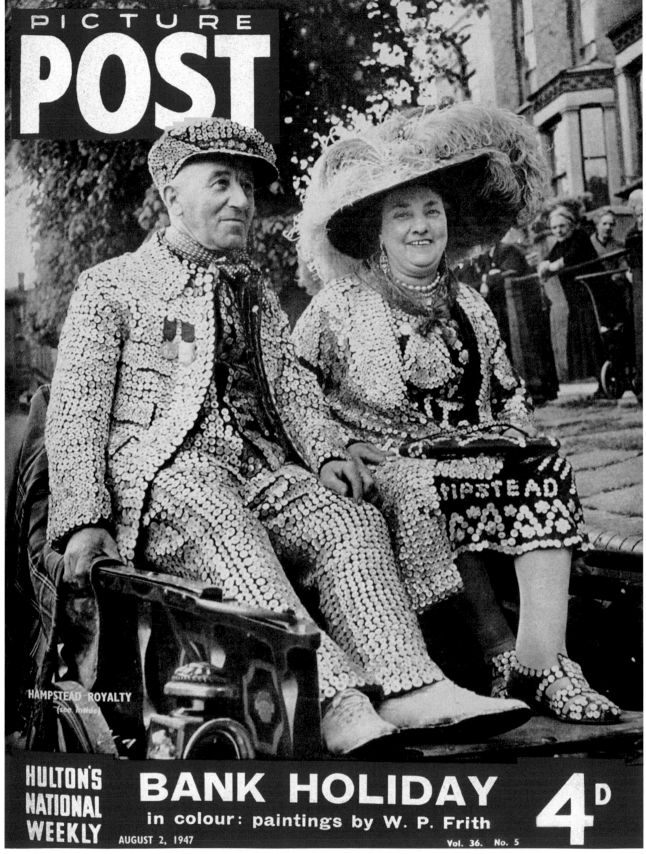

Hitler, Goebbels, Goering and Julius Steicher with those of their victims, selecting well-known Jewish scientists, writers and actors. This was a stunning example of photographic discourse at the service of a cause. It was more effective than any written argument.

Eloquent Images

But the virulent stands taken by Hopkinson were antithetical to the conservatism of the magazine's owner, Edward G. Hulton. In January 1941 the special *Plan for Britain* issue appeared and immediately provoked fierce debate by proposing a reorganisation of the country after the war. Hopkinson's socialist views infuriated Hulton, who went so far as to accuse him in 1945 of using his magazine as an instrument of communist propaganda.

In 1950 a reportage on the Korean War by James Cameron and Bert Hardy, commissioned by Hopkinson, related how the South Koreans, with the consent of the Americans, treated political prisoners who opposed the tyrannical Synghman Rhee. For Hulton, criticising the allies was tantamount to direct support of the communists. It was the last straw. Hopkinson was sacked, and replaced by Ted Castle. Several journalists, including James Cameron, Lionel Birch and A. L. Lloyd refused to work for *Picture Post* anymore, considering that muzzled in such a manner the magazine had lost its *raison d'être*.

Rise and Fall

Since the Second World War, sales of *Picture Post* had never stopped growing. In December 1943 it was selling 950,000 copies a week. Sales had reached 1,380,000 when Hopkinson left in 1950. By June 1952 they were down to 935,000 and continued to fall. The last issue was published in May 1957, selling only 600,000 copies.

Over a period of thirty years, *Picture Post* compiled a formidable archive, with more than 9,000 photo reportages, of which 4,000 were published, made up of the work of forty photographers, who forever marked the illustrated press with their exceptional expressive power.

PICTURE POST

KAISER ADOLF: The Man Against Europe

HULTON'S NATIONAL WEEKLY

In this issue:

BETWEEN PEACE AND WAR

SEPTEMBER 9, 1939

Vol. 4. No. 10

3D

PICTURE POST

HOW TO TREAT DICTATORS
Charlie Chaplin (left) in his new film "The Great Dictator"

HULTON'S NATIONAL WEEKLY

In this issue:

MOTOR TORPEDO BOATS

SEPTEMBER 14, 1940

Vol. 8. No. 11

3D

The New Market of Eroticism

The eldest son of a conservative Protestant family, good looking, with a diploma from the Art Institute of Chicago and an IQ of 152, Hugh Marston Hefner, Hef to his friends, had all it took to revolutionise the men's press, and indeed the sexual attitudes of America itself! In 1951 he became editor of *Esquire,* and in 1953 decided to launch his own magazine, based on a very simple idea: add a dose of sex to a traditional men's magazine. 'I never intended to be a revolutionary', he later claimed. But revolutionary he was.

Daring *Playboy*

The first issue of *Playboy* appeared in December 1953, with Marilyn Monroe on the cover. Of course the photograph itself was already well known, and Marilyn, sex symbol that she was, had already become part of America's cultural heritage. But no one else yet put a woman with such a plunging neckline on the cover of a magazine. The day that the first issue appeared, Hef did not even know if he would have the means to produce a second one. It sold like hotcakes: 55,000 copies! It was more than he had dared hope for.

The magazine's content was carefully balanced to appeal to a wide readership. Not only did the most famous women, alongside sumptuous models, display their charms, but there was also a good deal of material for those who actually wished to read it.

Over the years a host of great literary names have been invited to pen contributions, including Lenny Bruce, John Updike, Jack Kerouac, Joyce Carol Oates, Tom Clancy, Kurt Vonnegut, Saul Bellow, Stanley Elkin, Margaret Atwood, and even, in March 1960, Ian Fleming, with an adventure of a certain James Bond.

By the second issue the magazine had found its now famous logo, the little rabbit, hastily sketched by the suitably named Art Director,

1. Collage, Beatrice Paul. Photo, Pompeo Posar, September 1966. Art Director, Arthur Paul. 2. Cover, Robert Harmon, July 1972. 3. Photo, Pompeo Posar, October 1963. 4. Photo, Peter Winfield, December 1973-January 1974. Art Director, Arthur Paul.

3

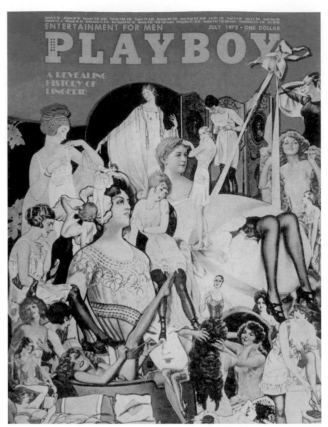

1

2

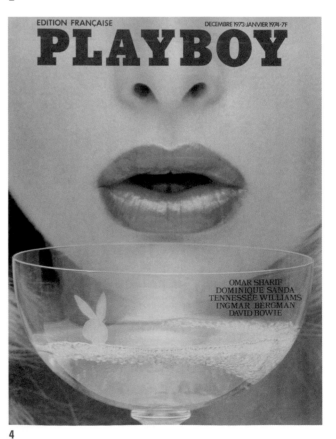

4

5

6

7

8

Arthur 'Art' Paul. Why a rabbit? Because of its hot sexual reputation perhaps. Its bowtie recalls the dinner jacket it wore in its original version. In 1959 the chic rabbit had become so famous that if a reader were to send a letter to the magazine with just the rabbit in the place of an address, it would still reach its destination!

Saucy French *Lui*

Playboy had shown the way and *Lui* followed in November 1963, adapting its formula for the French public. The women depicted were more mysterious than buxom, more elegant than provocative. Under the artistic direction of Pagnez and the photographer and editor Giacobetti, a master in the genre, slick highly coloured covers were produced, playing with effects of surprise rather than crude sexuality (2). Carefully designed, innovative in their staging and layout, they gave women an image that was both sexy and playful, proud of their seductive power without debasing themselves. Their bodies were bared just enough to suggest the rest, erotic as opposed to pornographic. For the first time even film actresses such as Mireille Darc agreed to be delicately undressed for the camera. Just like *Playboy,* a considerable amount of space was reserved for illustrators, notably Sam Aslan, who produced the airbrushed pin-up of the month. Between pages devoted to pretty girls there appeared articles by Romain Gary and Philippe Labro, to name but two. It was a real news magazine too, aimed at trendy executives with an open mind.

Its success was phenomenal and contributed to the rise of the Filipacchi publishing group. The magazine always steered a fine path, using superlative graphic design to give eroticism an intellectual touch, saving it from the lewd and vulgar depths of some of its successors.

5. Cover, Louis, 1st quarter 1960. **6.** Cover, Francis Giacobetti, 30th November 1965. **7.** Cover, Frank Gitti, April 1965. **8.** Cover, Frank Gitti, January 1967.

British Humour

Mr Punch is the comic puppet character descended from the Commedia del'Arte's Pulcinella. But from 1842 to 1992 *Punch* was also the title of a weekly satirical journal published in London and just as unbearable for those on the receiving end of its barbs. Also called *The London Charivari,* it followed in the same vein as the French daily *Le Charivari,* founded by Philippon in 1832, where the illustrator Daumier cut his teeth. The 1830s had also produced such titles as *Figaro in London* in 1831, edited first by Gilbert Abbott Beckett then by Henry Mayhew, who would go on to found *Punch; Punchinello* in 1832, illustrated by George Cruikshank; *Punch in London* by Mark Lemon, who would soon join the more concisely named *Punch*; and Thomas Hood's annual publication, *Comic Offering.*

Inspiration from Paris

In June 1841, having remarked upon the great success of *Le Charivari* in Paris, the artist and wood engraver Ebenezer Landells suggested to Henry Mayhew, a well-known journalist, that they adapt the concept to the London public. Mayhew met Mark Lemon, a very popular journalist, playwright and humorist. Sharing the same left-wing political outlook and brand of humour, all they needed was to find the rest of the team. They were soon joined by Douglas Jerrold, a journalist known for his fight on behalf of the poor, and received written contributions from Shirley Brooks, William Wills and William Makepeace Thackeray. The illustrators included John Leech, a medical student and a dab hand with a pencil who was with them from the beginning; Richard Doyle, who produced the cover illustration in 1849 which would be used until 1956; Archibald Henning; John Tenniel, the illustrator of Lewis Carroll's books, and one of the most prominent illustrators of the time, Charles Keene, who contributed from 1851 and joined the team in 1860, while George Du Maurier produced some work for the journal in 1860, and then joined them permanently from 1864. Later on *Punch* called on the talents of Harry Furniss, Linley Sambourne, Francis Carruthers Gould and

8—14 OCTOBER 1975   25p WEEKLY

This week : DOING HER OWN THING

2

3

4

5

Phil May. The first edition appeared on Saturday 17th July 1841. The magazine defined itself as 'a defender of the oppressed and a radical scourge of all authority'. Its prime targets were politicians, corrupt judges and the monarchy, accused of being too costly.

In December 1842 *Punch* was selling just 6,000 copies a week; 10,000 were needed to break even. It was bought out by the publishers and printers Bradbury and Evans whose stable included Charles Dickens. This provided the perfect opportunity for the editorial team to cosy up to the great novelist. They were both critical of the government and shared concern for the plight of the poor and dispossessed.

Biting Truth

Punch was a resolutely campaigning journal, using humour to violently denounce social injustice. In 1843, it published Thomas Hood's poem *The Song of the Shirt,* a searing diatribe against capitalism. From February 1846 until 1847 it ran Thackeray's serial entitled *The Snobs of England, by One of Themselves,* which was a great success.

By 1850 the journal had started to lose its bite, adapting itself to its readership, the growing middle class of conservative persuasion. From a commercial point of view its heyday came in the 1940s when it sold as many as 175,000 copies. Then followed a long decline, with closure coming in 1992. *Punch* was resuscitated at considerable expense four years later by Harrods's owner Mohamed Al-Fayed, but the journal, badly distributed and with a dwindling readership (down to 6,000 at the end) was obliged to give up the ghost in June 2002.

1. Margaret Thatcher. 8th to 14th October 1975. **2.** 2nd April 1924. **3.** Diana. 13th November 1985. **4.** Elisabeth Taylor and Richard Burton. 5. Frank Sinatra. 23rd to 29th June 1971.

Gift Wrapped Fascism

talian Fascism, like Communism or Nazism was a form of totalitarianism. Totalitarianism requires complete subservience to the state by an entire population, who are forced not only to obey but to believe in an ideology whose strict interpretation is limited to a small number of people, or even just one person. Contrary to traditional dictators interested only in their own power, Mussolini and the Fascists wanted the Italian people to embrace their movement, and to those ends put in place a propaganda machine equalled only by that of Soviet Russia.

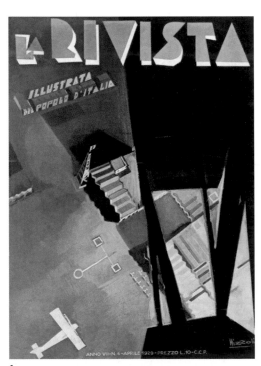

1

La Rivista had an interesting rôle in this organisation. Edited by Arnaldo Mussolini, Il Duce's own brother, it was a real family affair, and included articles by Margherita Sarfatti, Benito's mistress. *La Rivista illustrata del Popolo d'Italia* was the daily magazine founded by Mussolini when he was head of the Fascist Party before the March on Rome and his seizure of power in 1922. *La Rivista* was aimed at the country's intellectuals, a particularly difficult target. At the beginning, Fascism had seduced many intellectuals and

2

LA RIVISTA
ILLUSTRATA DEL POPOLO D'ITALIA

ANNO V°~ N°7~ LUGLIO 1927   PREZZO L.10~ C.C.P

3

artists, both in Italy and abroad. It was not by chance that the first Ministry of Culture in Western Europe (there was also one in Soviet Russia) was established under the Fascist regime.

Seeing itself as revolutionary and anti-conservative, Italian fascism attempted to garner support from avant-garde artists. One of these attempts was an article by Margherita Sarfatti in *La Rivista* on 6th June 1926 praising the work of Oskar Kokoschka, an Austrian painter who the Nazis would classify as a degenerate artist ten years later.

A Cultural Weapon

Exploiting the futurist movement, founded by Filippo Marinetti, *La Rivista* used its pictorial influence on the magazine's covers. It is interesting to note the parallel destinies of the painter Marinetti and the poet Maïakovski, childhood friends converted to the anti-bourgeois revolution, both of whom worked for the totalitarian regimes of their respective countries, one fascist, the other communist.

Of course the hopes of both the people and the intellectuals would be dashed. The imposture of both forms of totalitarianism would reveal itself several years after they came to power. Creative freedom proved incompatible, despite all attempts to demonstrate the contrary.

1. Illustration, Nizzoli, April 1929. **2.** Illustration, Giali Mondaini, June 1929. **3.** Illustration, Fabiani, July 1927.

Rock Life

In the beginning, *Rolling Stone* was just a fanzine, produced and distributed by a student, 21-year old Jann Wenner Was, in San Francisco. The eponymous magazine would become not only the essential rock 'n' roll magazine, but also the first to reach such a wide public, treating rock music as a true element of culture, another way of seeing the world.

Vehicle of Counter-Culture

The first unimpressive looking issue appeared in 1967, printed on cheap paper. The cover bore a photo of John Lennon, but dressed as a soldier. The 'peace and love' campaigner was snapped in costume on the set of the film *How I Won the War*. The tone of the magazine would be original, unconventional and not swayed by the star system. The title was inspired by the name of a group that were well on their way to success, The Rolling Stones, whose singer, Mick Jagger, would grace the cover nineteen times. The magazine soon became so successful that the stars rushed to make its cover, including The Beatles, Bob Dylan, Tina Turner, Eric Clapton, Frank Zappa, Rod Stewart, Diane Keaton, Jane Fonda and even the Incredible Hulk.

Some of the hottest photographers have worked for the magazine, including Annie Leibovitz, Francesco Scavullo, Herb Ritts, Richard Avdeon, Matthew Rolston, Albert Watson, Mark Seliger and Anton Corbjin. One illustrious illustrator was none other than Andy Warhol. The layout was psychedelic, with articles by Tom Wolfe or Hunter S. Thomson, while John Lennon and Yoko Ono also provided material. In the first issue Wenner announced: '*Rolling Stone* will not only deal with music, but also the attitudes that this music contains'. The hippy generation finally had a magazine for themselves, a magazine that moved with the times. With an initial print run of 6,000, the bimonthly now sells 1.25 million copies.

1. John Lennon and Yoko Ono. 22nd January 1981. 2. Mick Jagger. 11th September 1975. 3. Robert Redford and Dustin Hoffman. 8th April 1976. 4. Mohamed Ali. 4th May 1978. 5. O.J. Simpson. 8th September 1977.

1

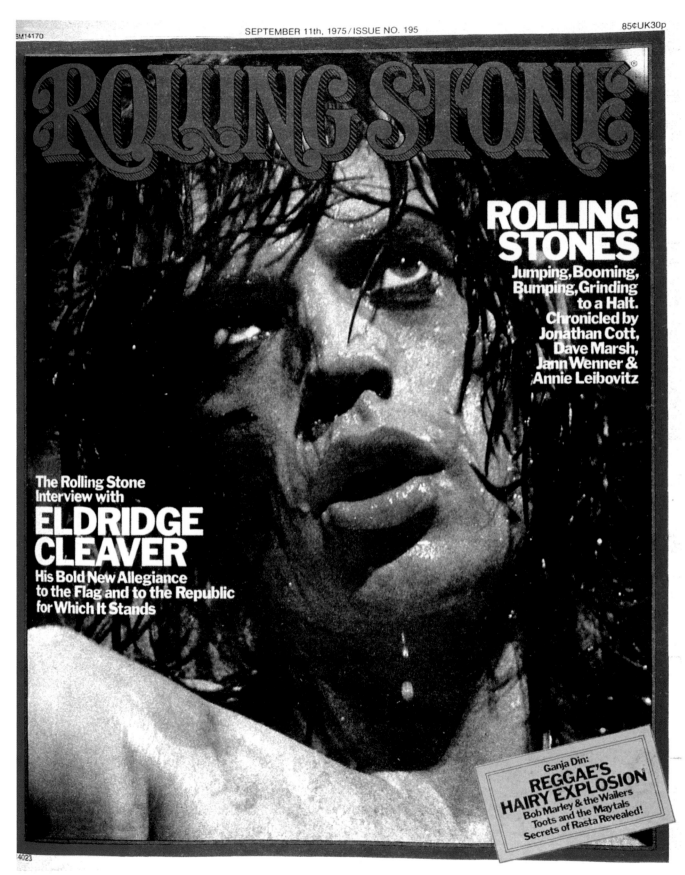

SEPTEMBER 11th, 1975 / ISSUE NO. 195

85¢UK30p

ROLLING STONE®

ROLLING STONES

Jumping, Booming, Bumping, Grinding to a Halt. Chronicled by Jonathan Cott, Dave Marsh, Jann Wenner & Annie Leibovitz

The Rolling Stone Interview with

ELDRIDGE CLEAVER

His Bold New Allegiance to the Flag and to the Republic for Which It Stands

Ganja Din:
REGGAE'S HAIRY EXPLOSION
Bob Marley & the Wailers
Toots and the Maytals
Secrets of Rasta Revealed!

2

DANIEL SCHORR'S Journal of a Dark Season: Seventeen Months on the CIA Watch

RollingStone

TWO-STAR FINAL
Robert Redford and Dustin Hoffman Dismantle the Presidency by Chris Hodenfield

WARHOL Snags LOU REED

3

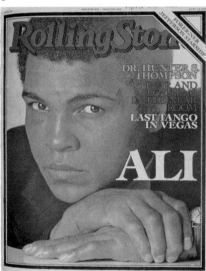

DR. HUNTER S. THOMPSON FEAR AND LOATHING IN THE LOCKER ROOM
LAST TANGO IN VEGAS

ALI

4

THE JUICE
OJ Simpson
A Man for All Seasons
By Tim Cahill

HI-FI '78
Sex Symbols & Their Sound Effects
10 Super Systems
Betamax: The Video Wars
Mono Nostalgia and More

5

America's Reflection

The *Saturday Evening Post* is considered to be the oldest American magazine, since it is the direct descendant of the *Pennsylvania Gazette,* founded by Benjamin Franklin in 1728. The first issue to bear the title *The Saturday Evening Post* dates from 4th August 1821. It was a four page journal without illustrations, published by Atkinson & Alexander. In 1839 George Rex Graham turned it into a journal that was 'family oriented, politically neutral, morally respectful, devoted to literature and national and foreign news'. At the end of the 1890s it encountered serious financial problems. Cyrus H. Curtis, owner of the *Ladies Home Journal*, bought it in 1897. It reappeared the following year, with an editorial line centred on three subjects – the economy, politics and literature – and a new design incorporating many illustrations.

Only the Finest

In 1899, Curtis hired Georges Horace Lorimer as literary editor. He hired the best journalists, including Frank Norris, David Graham Phillips, Willa Cather and Jack London, as well as printing the work of writers such as Rudyard Kipling, Sinclair Lewis or H. G. Wells. The greatest illustrators also graced its pages,

1

2

3

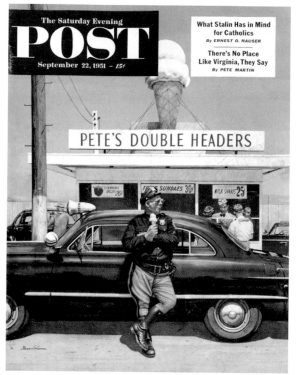

4

5

6

particularly Norman Rockwell, who produced more than three hundred covers in 47 years of close collaboration with the journal, as well as Joseph C. Leyendecker, Charles Marion Russell, Walter Everett, John Clymer, Stevan Dohanos, Sarah Stilwell-Weber and John LaGatta.

Although circulation was down to 2,000 at the time of the buyout, it was over a million in 1908 and double that figure in 1913. More commercial and with wider appeal than *The New Yorker,* it became an institution, representing America's growing middle-class.

Change of Direction

It started to lose its readers during the 1930s however, when Lorimer transformed this leisure magazine into a political organ. Just as the magazine garnered unprecedented success when it published the writings of F. Scott Fitzgerald or William Faulkner, its conservatism now provoked its decline, at a time when the *The New Yorker* and its avant-garde humour was really taking off. In 1936, Ben Hibbs succeeded George H. Lorimer. He changed the format of the magazine, as well as the cover layout, getting rid of the band across the top, therefore freeing the whole of the cover for the illustration that made the magazine so distinctive.

In 1947 the production cost of each issue was valued at thirty cents, more than double its retail price, and so its economic survival depended on advertising. In 1960 it was selling six million copies a week.

In December 1963 the decision was taken to abandon the principle of a cover illustration in a vain attempt at modernisation. Gradually the magazine became unprofitable, and ceased publication in February 1969.

1. Illustration, Constantin Alajalov, 12th March 1949. Art Director, Kenneth Stuart. 2. Illustration, Norman Rockwell, 15th December 1945. 3. Illustration, Norman Rockwell, 9th July 1949. Art Director, Kenneth Stuart. 4. Illustration, Stevan Dohanos, 22nd September 1951. Art Director, Kenneth Stuart. 5. Illustration, Hugues, 29th November 1952. Art Director, Kenneth Stuart. 6. Illustration, Stevan Dohanos, 2nd February 1952. Art Director, Kenneth Stuart.

Insolence at the Tip of a Pencil

In 1896 Albert Langen, son of a German industrialist, launched a new satirical magazine, *Simplicissimus*. He started by recruiting the illustrator who gave its covers such a particularly original look, Thomas Heine. Originally a painter, and Jewish, Heine had also produced illustrations for magazines like *Fliegende Blatter* or *Die Jugend,* with a predilection for caricature. He did not hide his dislike of the Far Right. Although the magazine welcomed such distinguished writers as Thomas Mann, Frank Wedekind or Rainer Maria Rilke, it stood out primarily for the originality of its graphics, with bright colours, very modern aesthetics and above all its many satirical drawings. Scenes from everyday life were sketched with an impertinence quite in tune with the German journalism of the time.

Disturbing Humour

Along with *Kladderadatsch,* the other satirical journal of the period (a weekly that claimed to appear 'daily except for working days'), *Simplicissimus* was a revolutionary publication. The government made its displeasure known. In 1897 the magazine defended the right to strike, despite the laws that had been passed banning it. The following year Wilhelm II, who had already opposed this kind of press which he deemed to be bad for Germany's image abroad, seized an issue of *Simplicissimus* that satirised the emperor's visit to Palestine. Albert Langen and Frank Wedekind, who had written the article in question, and Thomas Heine, who had lent his pen to their efforts, were sued. Albert Langen fled to Switzerland for five years, while the other two spent several months in prison for having attacked the monarchy.

The Norwegian cartoonist Olaf Gulbransson joined the team in 1902. His influence on the magazine would be considerable. He was soon followed by Rudolf Wilke, Walter Trier and Edward Thony. *Simplicissimus* continued to attack the establishment, to such an extent that the right-wing newspaper *Augsburger Postzeitung* accused it of constituting 'a real danger to school discipline'. Military discipline, with its exemplary punishments and special

1

2

3

4

1. Illustration, Wigg Siegl, 9ᵗʰ February 1963. **2.** Illustration, H. E. Köhler, 7ᵗʰ May 1955. **3.** Illustration, Josef Sauer, 9ᵗʰ April 1960. **4.** Illustration, Manfred Oesterle, 30ᵗʰ April 1960. **5.** Illustration, Manfred Oesterle, 16ᵗʰ March 1963.

Simplicissimus
B 6307 C   Jahrgang 1963 Nummer 11 — München, den 16. März 1963   Preis 75 Pfg.

Kleineuropäisches
Freundespaar

Zeichnung: Manfred Oesterle

privileges for high-ranking officers, was regularly derided. Religion was also a target. In 1906 the editor, Ludwig Thoma, spent six months in prison for an article that was a little too critical. These scandals only served as publicity. Circulation soon soared from 15,000 to 85,000 copies. When the king of Bavaria asked the authorities to ban a particular issue, he was advised that it was better not to, for fear of raising the profile of the rebellious journal even further. The left-wing press also attacked *Simplicissimus* for depicting workers as drunkards. In short, the magazine ruffled everyone's feathers. It became a private company in 1906, with its shareholders composed of the main members of its editorial staff, including Ludwig Thoma, Thomas Heine, Olaf Gulbransson, Rudolf Wilke and Edward Thony.

So Provocative

During the First World War, after much internal debate, the magazine decided that it would continue publication, but Ludwig Thoma, who joined the army in 1917, refuted this critical spirit he saw as being 'immature' and incompatible with the defence of a cause. After the war he joined a right-wing group and did not play an active role in the magazine from the 1920s onwards.

New illustrating talent arrived, including Karl Arnold, who became a shareholder, Erich Schilling, George Grosz and Kathe Kollwitz. Yet the magazine's circulation was down to just 30,000 copies on average, far from the 86,000 of 1914. It defended the Weimar Republic against the revolutionary Left and the nationalist Right, opposing Hitler in particular. When he came to power in 1933, Thomas Heine, whose caricatures had been less than kind to him, was forced to flee the country. The magazine survived the start of the Second World War, before its sarcastic laugh was extinguished in 1944.

5

Agent Provocateur

A *Stern* cover never leaves you indifferent. Everything is designed to catch the eye, from the yellow star on a red background that is its striking, aggressive logo – like a comic strip graphic where characters get punched in the face – to its shocking yet sumptuous photomontages. But once it has grabbed your attention it continues to draw you in, making you linger, curious to discover more; you are hooked, and *Stern* has bagged another reader.

In-Your-Face Covers

Computer-aided image processing creates audacious pictures that go straight to the heart of the matter. The cover on contaminated meat illustrates well the power of images over words: the skull and crossbones, symbol of danger, blends into the spots on the skin through skillful montage (7). It resembles stylised graffiti tags, or the marks with which cattle are branded, evoking the idea that these beasts are marked out as bearers of disease from their youngest age. One image says it all.

Visual Metaphors

Most montages serve as metaphors: the handle of a petrol pump that resembles the grip of a revolver depicts the economic suicide of President Carter's strong-arm tactics with the oil-producing countries (1). The morphing of the front of a plane into a skull addresses the subject of terrorism (8). Another cover shows men, nude like classical Greek statues, in an Atlas-like pose, bearing the weight not of the world but of two gigantic breasts. The irony lies in the fact that they are being crushed by the very woman fantasise about (2).
Another compositional trick consists of representing a turn of phrase through an image, such as in the literal depiction of the cold war (3), where all the hypocrisy of the handshake between Carter and Brezhnev – they aren't even looking at each other – is underlined by the icicles hanging off them.

Scoop and Shock

For more than half a century *Stern* has been the leading German magazine of the Burda

1

2

3

4

5

6

7

group, ahead of titles such as *Bunte, Neue Revue* and *Quick*. It never hesitates to provoke readers with crude or shocking covers. Eager to break exciting stories it has sometimes published scoops that turned out to be false. One of the most famous cases was a supposed diary of Hitler, in fact a fake document cobbled together in East Germany. With a circulation of more than a million *Stern* has a more popular readership than *Der Spiegel*, without the gutter-press element of *Bildzeitung*. A serious news magazine, it accords significant space to the image, publishing many spectacular photographs, often mixing beauty and brutality, by Rolf Gillhausen, Thomas Höpker, Robert Lebeck, Volker Hinz, Max Scheler, Stefan Moses, James Nachtwey, Michel Comte or Hans-Jürgen Burkard. It is part of the Grüner und Jahr group, which also publishes women's, and family periodicals, including *Brigitte, Eltern, Nicole, Essen und Trinken, Schöner wohnen* and *Geo*.

1. Photo, Michael Hospelt, 19th July 1979. **2.** 1973. **3.** Photo, Jacques Schumacher, 31st January 1980. **4.** Photo, Jan Michael, 15th February 1979. **5.** Photo, Nicholas Garland/The Spectator, after a painting by Niklaus Deutsch, 3rd March 1988. Art Director, Thomas Höpker. **6.** Photo, ZEFA, after a caricature by Felix Musil, 14th May 1981. **7.** Photo, Andrej Reiser/RI Kaiser, 18th August 1988. Art Director, Thomas Höpker. **8.** Photo, Klaus Böhle; illustration, Carl-W. Höhrig, 21st April 1988. Art Director, Thomas Höpker.

Serious and with it, the All-Embracing *Sunday Telegraph*

The first issue of the *Sunday Telegraph* appeared in London on the 5th of February 1961. This is how the new weekly presented itself to its readers: 'Today the first national Sunday newspaper for 40 years is published.' It was launched with the conviction that a pertinent Sunday paper did not exist for an enlightened Sunday readership. The *Sunday Telegraph* hoped to fill this gap. On one hand there were two serious and weighty newspapers that gave the appearance of being magazines, on the other there was a large number of sensationalist tabloids.

Standing Out

The *Sunday Telegraph* did not ignore the wide range of newspapers available to the public at the weekend. While deliberately restricting the number of pages so as to remain a reasonable size, it focussed on succinct reports and a coverage of national and international current affairs. For certain readers the *Sunday Telegraph* became 'the paper you can read from cover to cover', while for others it was 'the paper that satisfies'.

Although it denies the fact, the *Sunday Telegraph* was originally conceived as the Sunday edition of *The Daily Telegraph,* the illustrious daily from whence it came. But it benefited from an independent editorial team. Although it adopted the layout of its American peers – uncluttered pages, investigative journalism, colour photographs and free supplements – the number of copies sold (about 750,000) has never equalled that of *The Daily Telegraph* (roughly a million).

The Telegraph Group, a Prestigious History

Founded in 1855 by Colonel Sleigh, *The Daily Telegraph and Courier* was bought a month later by Joseph Levy, who was already the editor and owner of *The Sunday Times.* He ensured its rapid success by cutting its price to one penny. But it was Edward Levy Lawson, his son, who was the true architect of the paper's prosperity. Barely six years after its launch, the circulation was already twice that of *The Times*. The paper was thoroughly

1

2

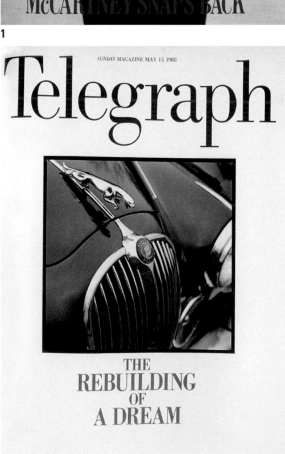

3

4

5

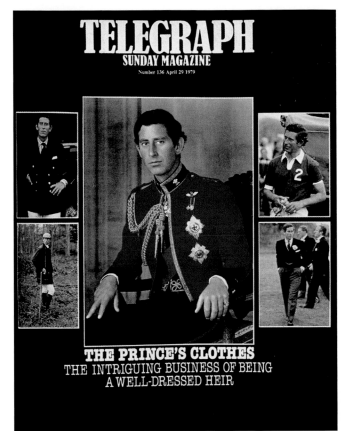

6

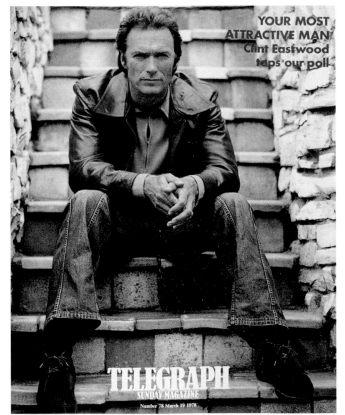

7

8

informed, well written and serious but without being boring. In 1875 it became the preferred daily of the middle class, who found *The Times* too daunting a read. Lawson was rewarded with a peerage, becoming Lord Burnham in 1903, while in 1914, two years before his death, the profession paid public homage to him, dubbing him 'Father of the Press'.

In the 1960s *The Daily Telegraph* was considered the virtually official voice of the Conservative Party. The Canadian multi-millionaire Conrad Black, who already owned a wide range of titles in Canada and the United States, bought *The Daily Telegraph* and *Sunday Telegraph* in 1985. The papers maintained their political orientation, however, with their principal readership being found among the prosperous middle class of Southeast England.

Since the 1990s the *Sunday Telegraph,* along with the rest of the Sunday press, has suffered from the growth of Saturday newspapers. Many of these now include magazines and special supplements. This vogue was launched by *The Daily Telegraph,* accompanied by *The Independent,* after they received permission to publish television and radio listings for the coming week. The success was considerable and sparked competition with the Sunday papers. Although in the 1990s the magazine began to focus more of its attention on celebrities, turning its back on the values expounded in its first issue, this change of direction may be explained, to a large extent at least, by market pressures.

1. Linda McCartney. 22nd February 1987. **2.** Audrey Hepburn. 20th May 1979. **3.** Jaguar. 15th May 1988. **4.** Anthony Perkins and Rod Steiger. 30th September 1984. **5.** Bob Hope. 20th January 1977. **6.** Prince Charles. 29th April 1979. **7.** Clint Eastwood. 19th March 1978. **8.** Peter O'Toole. 24th August 1980.

Overleaf
9. Margaret Thatcher. 21st August 1983. **10.** The warders of the Tower of London. 12th March 1978.

TELEGRA
NDAY MAGAZINE

BRITISH GOTHIC
We add our own
parody to the many
other copies of
America's most famous
painting

Number 358 August 21 1983

TELEGRAPH
SUNDAY MAGAZINE

The Tower of London –
Nine Centuries of Grandeur
Number 77 March 12 1978

10

The Sunday Revolution

The first British weekly to come out on a Sunday was the *Sunday Monitor* in 1779, which survived until 1829. In 1791 *The Observer* was born; Henry White launched the *New Observer* in 1821 as a direct competitor. The rivalry between the two papers proved to be long and fierce, although White's venture was initially less than successful, despite changing the name a few months later to *The Independent Observer*. He got it right third time around though, adopting the name *The Sunday Times* in October 1822, an allusion to *The Times* (founded in 1785). The paper changed hands a number of times and at one point was run by Rachel Beer, whose husband owned *The Observer*. However, the great names in its history are undoubtedly those of the Berry brothers (Lords Camrose and Kemsley), who started its foreign circulation in 1915, and Roy Thomson, who acquired the paper in 1959.

A Daring Venture

At the beginning of 1961, Thomson announced his great idea: to launch a free colour magazine which would be included with the paper, so opening up a completely new advertising market and widening the readership by attracting the children of the current readers. The idea was very badly received. 'Free?'

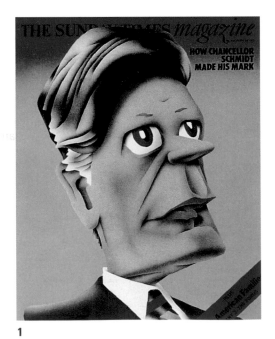

1

2

Chairman of China

3

THE COURT OF PICASSO

5

6

'Young people?' 'Colour!' 'It won't last three months!' But Denis Hamilton, the editor, also believed in the idea, declaring, 'I don't want this magazine to interest people who are in their eighties!' He formed a new team of 'rebel' thirty-year olds, 'a mix of pop journalists and intellectuals' headed by Mark Boxer, and insisted on the top graphic designers, poaching Michael Rand from the *Daily Express* as art director. The British press was to undergo a revolution, despite a rather slippery start. After the launch in February 1962 Hamilton received 1,200 letters protesting this excess of modernity. He answered them all personally, writing of his four children. But *The Sunday Times Magazine* was spurned by advertisers and mocked by its rivals. Full colour printing, it was thought, would result in financial ruin.

But in January 1963, when only the previous October Thomson had spoken of 'suicide', the happy news was announced that advertising sales had reached 1 million pounds. The whole team and a clutch of guests jetted off to Moscow to celebrate the first anniversary of this exciting venture. The 'colour supplement', as it was called until 1964 when it became a 'magazine', had already reeled in 150,000 extra sales per week. Their once-mocking competitors had no choice but to copy them. *The Telegraph Magazine* appeared in January 1964, followed by *The Observer Magazine* in September.

Smart Moves

Godfrey Smith succeeded Mark Boxer as editor of the magazine, affirming that 'we are one of the only primarily visual magazines'. Under his stewardship the content shifted towards social themes and away from fashion. His team, including Donad McCullin, Snowdon, Ray Green and Philip Jones-Griffiths, dared to tackle social subjects through hard-hitting photojournalism. In 1967 the paper merged with *The Times*, bought a year before by Lord Thomson. Both titles were then sold to Rupert Murdoch in 1981. The circulation of the *The Sunday Times* today stands at 1.3 million and the magazine has spawned separate culture and style supplements.

1. Helmut Schmidt. 16th November 1975. 2. Idi Amin Dada. 28th December 1975. 3. 10th August 1969. 4. Mao Tse-Tung. 23rd March 1969. 5. Humphrey Bogart. 18th October 1970. 6. Pablo Picasso. 25th April 1965.

Fashion and Glamour

From its launch in the early 20th century, *Tatler* won over its female readers through pertinent coverage of British society. Alongside articles covering new subjects and written in the latest style, was the more traditional fare of fashion photographs and pictures of stars of the stage and screen. This successful blend of celebrity news and more detailed investigations of the tastes and trends of the English society lady would be the key to the success of *Tatler*. The era of the Rolling Stones and The Beatles also left its mark. Like all of its competitors, *Tatler* turned towards fashion and entertainment. Yet perhaps we should also remember the ghost of the first English journal to be called *Tatler*, published first in April 1709 in London by Sir Richard Steele, writer, dramatist, essayist and politician.

Tatler, Two Hundred Years Earlier

Inform and entertain were the editorial watchwords of Steele's journal. Using the pseudonym Isaac Bickerstaff for his reports, the scene was always either his own apartment or one of the numerous London coffee or chocolate houses. He mixed a subtle blend of aesthetic and literary commentary with anecdotes that served his purpose of instructing society in the precepts that every perfect gentleman or lady should respect. In today's *Tatler*, part of the Condé Nast Group, which also owns *Vanity Fair, Vogue, Glamour* and *The New Yorker*, the coffee houses have been usurped by Miami Beach, Rome or Paris, and discussion of correct deportment has given way to glamour photos of models promoting merits of high fashion and beauty creams. Times have certainly changed.

1. 17th June 1925. 2. 5th May 1965. 3. Teresa Manners photographed by Herb Ritts. 4. 30th June 1965.

THE TATLER, JUNE 17, 1925

POSTAGE RATES, SEE FRONTISPIECE

VOL. XCVI., No. 1251

The Tatler

Summer № 1/-

REGISTERED AS A NEWSPAPER FOR TRANSMISSION IN THE UNITED KINGDOM.

1

2

3

4

The Most Famous Fashion Magazine

The first issue of *Vogue* appeared in America in 1892. It was a weekly society gazette, created by Arthur Baldwin Turnure, with fashion as its central subject, alongside short stories and poetry. Lacking advertisers, the magazine widened its scope. Although its reputation was based essentially on its *haute couture* features, it started to include more and more reports on the less expensive ready-to-wear. After Turnure died in 1906 the magazine was managed collectively, then bought by Condé Nast in 1909. It changed its format, became a bimonthly and focussed much more on its covers, which were now in colour, produced by Helen Dryden, Eduardo Benito, Georges Lepape or Carl Erickson.

Luxury, Fashion and Sensuality

Vogue was distributed in Europe through a German agency. It was a success, particularly since local publishing was greatly disrupted by the war. In 1916, however, export became impossible. So the British version of *Vogue* was born. Thanks to its editor Dorothy Todd, who was very involved with the Bloomsbury group, the magazine acquired a reputation for being intellectually avant-garde. In 1920 the first French edition appeared, printed in London and edited by Michel de Brunhoff. The magazine gained even more prestige, attracting the cream of the Art Deco artists. Although its articles were light, the accompanying illustrations were of the highest quality. Photography, treated like painting with veils of mist or smoke, favored the pictorial aesthetic that had been made fashionable by Adolf de Meyer.

In 1923 the future great couturier Main Bocher joined the American team, as did the photographer Edward Steichen, who replaced Meyer's artistic flourishes with a geometrical rigour. A few years later Cecil Beaton would shift the balance towards a more surreal atmosphere, making *Vogue* a chronicler of the history of modern art. The attempt to launch a German *Vogue* failed in 1928, while the American edition struggled through the crash of 1929. But the visual quality was maintained,

1

1. Cover, Blumenfeld/Gruau, 1st April 1954. Art Director, Alexander Liberman. **2.** Cover, Horst, 15th May 1943. Art Director, Alexander Liberman. **3.** Cover, John Rawling, 1st June 1947. Art Director, Alexander Liberman. **4.** Cover, Blumenfeld, 1st August 1953. Art Director, Alexander Liberman.

Overleaf
Selection of covers from the most famous fashion magazine: the different faces of Vogue.

Beauty Issue

How to

Look your best

Feel your best

Do your best

MAY 15, 1943
PRICE 35 CENTS

40 CENTS IN CANADA

COPYRIGHT 1943, THE CONDÉ NAST PUBLICATIONS INC.

3

4

with the participation of photographers such as Horst, Durst, Bruehl and Blumenfeld, and illustrators including Vertès, Boët-Willaumez and Bérard. Publication was again affected when the the Second World War broke out. The English edition was much reduced, the French edition disappeared completely and the American edition, starved of news from the Parisian catwalks, became more American. When Condé Nast died in 1942 he was replaced by Iva Patcevitch, who made Alex Libermann, the former editor of *Vu*, art director. Under his aegis the magazine worked with photographers like Irving Penn, Toni Frissell, William Klein or Jerry Schatzberg.

Fashionable Photographers

In January 1945 co-operation with Paris was re-established. From 1962 to 1971, with Diana Vreeland at the helm, it developed even further, becoming more kitsch through the influence of pop art, and more aggressive, with the work of photographers such as Richard Avedon, Helmut Newton, Bob Richardson and David Bailey. It returned to neo-romanticism and spontaneity in the 1970s, under the guidance of Grace Mirabella, who called upon the talent of Duane Michals, Arthur Elgort, Chris von Wangenheim, Sarah Moon and Deborah Turbeville. Today, *Vogue's* empire includes seven luxuriant editions, printed on glossy paper.

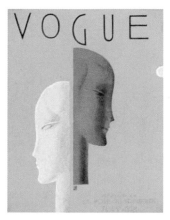

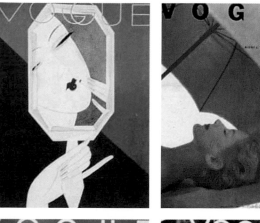

Breaking New Ground

The French poet Louis Aragon described *Vu* as 'a magazine such as you've never seen before, the first major illustrated magazine in the world.' And he was right. When Lucien Vogel founded this news magazine with so many pages devoted to photography, the formula already existed in Germany, but not in France.

Born in 1886, the son of an illustrator known for his caricatures, particularly in *L'Assiette au beurre,* Lucien Vogel became a journalist at the age of twenty-two. Editor of *La Gazette du bon ton* and *Jardin des modes* and art director of the French edition of *Vogue* until 1925 and *Fémina,* he would overturn the visual habits of the French by making the image 'speak'. As its name indicates, *Vu* was a magazine that lent itself more to viewing than reading. 70 to 80% of its pages were devoted to photography. The greatest names and rising young talent all participated in its success, including André Kertesz, Robert Capa, Man Ray, Germaine Krull, Brassaï, Henri Cartier-Bresson, who had his first photo reportage published in *Vu*, and of course Marie-Claude Vaillant-Couturier, under the pseudonym of Marivo, Vogel's daughter, who published the

1

2

3

4

5

6

first report on the concentration camps. In her own words: 'At *Vu,* the only instructions given to photographers were to go to such and such a place. They did what they liked, taking the photographs they wished.' A free hand was also given to the layout artists, as she explains: 'At the time, composition still used lead, but we printed proofs on cellulose paper called a cello-text. So the layout artists only had flexible materials with which to work – cello-texts and photographic film – to lay out their pages. That probably explains their unbounded creativity; they broke out of the confining box of vertical columns, making anything possible.'

Say it with Pictures

Photomontage also enabled multiple compositions, the speciality of the art director Alexandre Liebermann (4, 7, 8), a painter and sculptor, trained in the cubist school, and future art director of *Vogue*. The editor Carlo Rim used modern writers such as Philippe Soupault, but the strongpoint of the journal remained the reportage, striking images that were neither vulgar nor decorative. Photographers were finally given the status of artists and could sign their work. This was also the first time that a magazine used snapshots to such a huge extent, taken by reporters using the Leica, the best of the new small, light and silent cameras that appeared at the time. It gave the news a whole new look.

According to press records for the years 1932 to 1937, *Vu* was read by half a million families. In 1936, because of financial difficulties, the magazine was sold to Albert Mallet. The style and tone changed, accompanied by a fall in the quality of both form and content. The readership dropped and publication ceased in March 1938.

1. Cover, Tabard, 2nd October 1929. **2.** Cover, Tabard and Vie à la Campagne, 23rd November 1932. **3.** *V.* Eleanor Parker. Cover, Warner Bros First National, 2nd February 1947. **4.** Photo, SAAD; montage, Alexandre Liebermann, 8th November 1933. **5.** Cover, Landau and Kertesz, 29th June 1932. **6.** 31st August 1938.

Overleaf
7. Photo SAAD; montage, Alexandre Liebermann, 5th July 1933. **8.** Montage, Alexandre Liebermann, 3rd March 1934.

VU LOR

669 - 02

LA CHUTE D'UN DIEU

5 JUILLET 1933
6ᵉ ANNÉE. — Nᵒ 277
PRIX : 6 FRANCS
PARAIT LE MERCREDI
Directeur : LUCIEN VOGEL
Photo SAAD · Montage d'ALEXANDRE

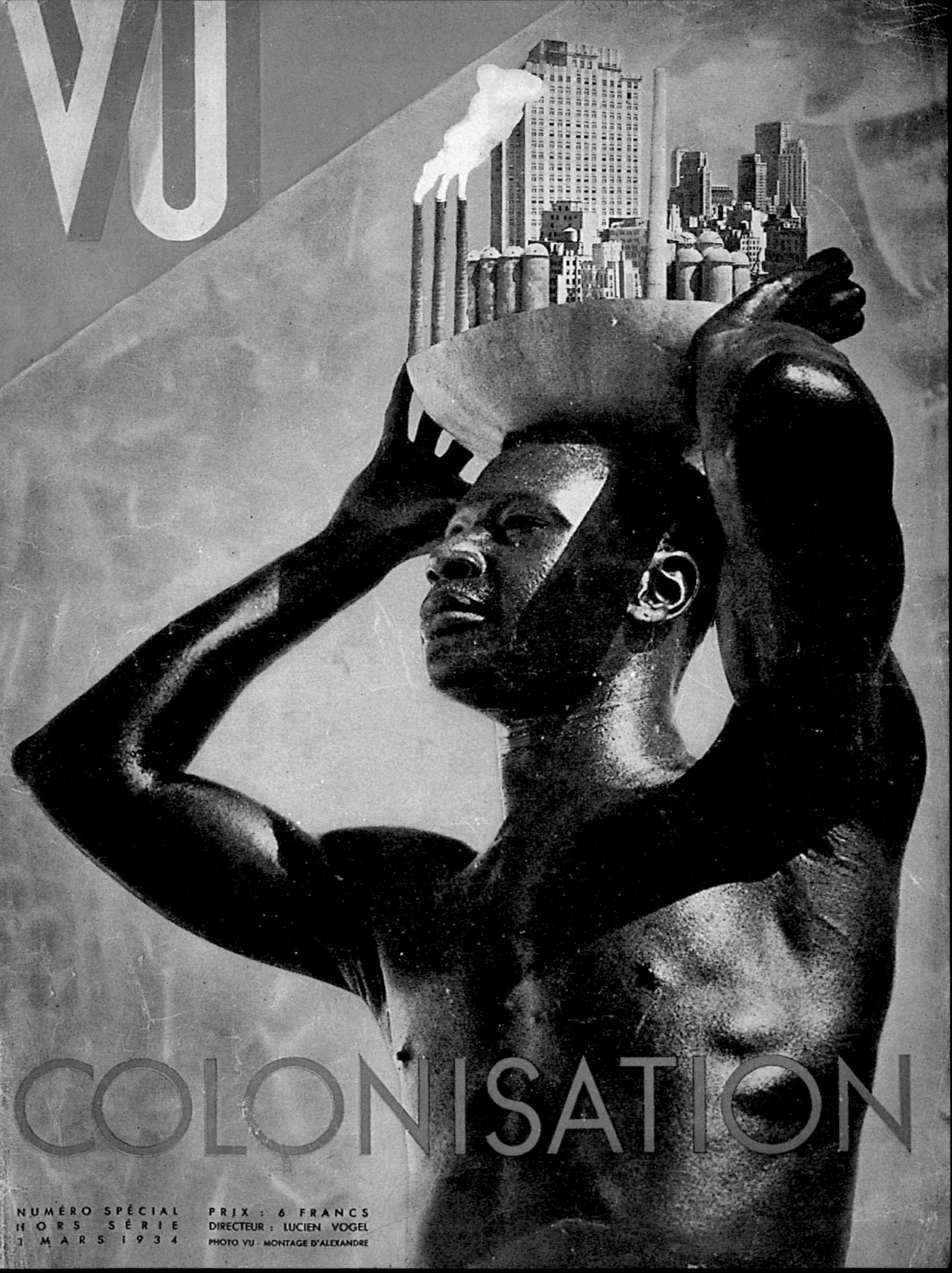

VU

COLONISATION

NUMÉRO SPÉCIAL
HORS SÉRIE
1 MARS 1934

PRIX : 6 FRANCS
DIRECTEUR : LUCIEN VOGEL
PHOTO VU · MONTAGE D'ALEXANDRE

90

TRENDS

This chapter traces some of the major trends in graphics, from the golden age of caricature to Pop Art, including the explosion of the kitsch style and other graphic effects and fashions which were popular in their time.

From this we develop several themes of note linked to geopolitical events such as wars, or social phenomena - for example, transport, sport or fashion.

Finally we look at the people who have set the records for the most appearances on covers, taking them in alphabetical order from Brigitte Bardot to Stalin. These most popular characters are stars of show-biz or politics, victims of the paparazzi (Princess Diana), or those who control their own image (Madonna), those who needed to shine (Grace Kelly) or simply by nature (Marilyn Monroe), variations on a single theme (Hitler) or people ambiguous right down to their image (Stalin).

Time: the Most Copied Magazine in the World

Founded in 1923 by the future press magnate Henry R. Luce and his friend Britton Hadden, the magazine *Time Weekly News* was designed to provide news to the harried business-man. Each issue consisted of around a hundred articles, all of them hardly longer than a page, summarised from the New York *Times.* It was a huge and immediate success. Three years after its launch it was selling 110,000 copies a week and double that by 1929. Anatole Grunwald, who was hired by Hedley Donovan in 1963 after Luce's death, wanted a 'more intelligent and more intellectual' publication. Although he remodelled the magazine, its political orientation remained resolutely Republican. Today it has a print run of 6 million.

The Famous Border

Like many good ideas the design for the cover of *Time* was a simple one: a red border, like a red marker pen underlining essential information. 'Important!' it seemed to shout. 'A must read!' it called, catching the eye of the busy man scurrying past. Initially the border was employed to confer an almost iconic status on the subject matter (2), reinforcing the 'serious' position of the magazine, particularly since it also served to frame the portraits of the personalities that graced the covers, like that of an oil painting. Later the red border was used much more subtly, often as a background, enabling such trompe-l'œils as in (1) where it serves as a sort of wall on which the image is riveted. The picture budget of the magazine is colossal, its business supporting several agencies in their entirety and paying up to 50,000 dollars for a single photograph. This visual concept of the red border has been copied by *L'Express* in France (3), *Der Spiegel* in Germany (4) and countless other publications.

1. *Time.* Willy Brandt. Sculpture in steel and aluminium by George Giusti. Art Director, Louis R. Glessmann. 4th January 1971. 2. *Time.* Cover (Stalin), Ernest Hamlin Baker, 1st January 1940. 3. *L'Express.* Cover (Pope Pius XII), Holmes, 26th October to 1st November 1964. Art Director, André Gobert. 4. *Der Spiegel.* Nikita Khrushchev. 17th July 1957.

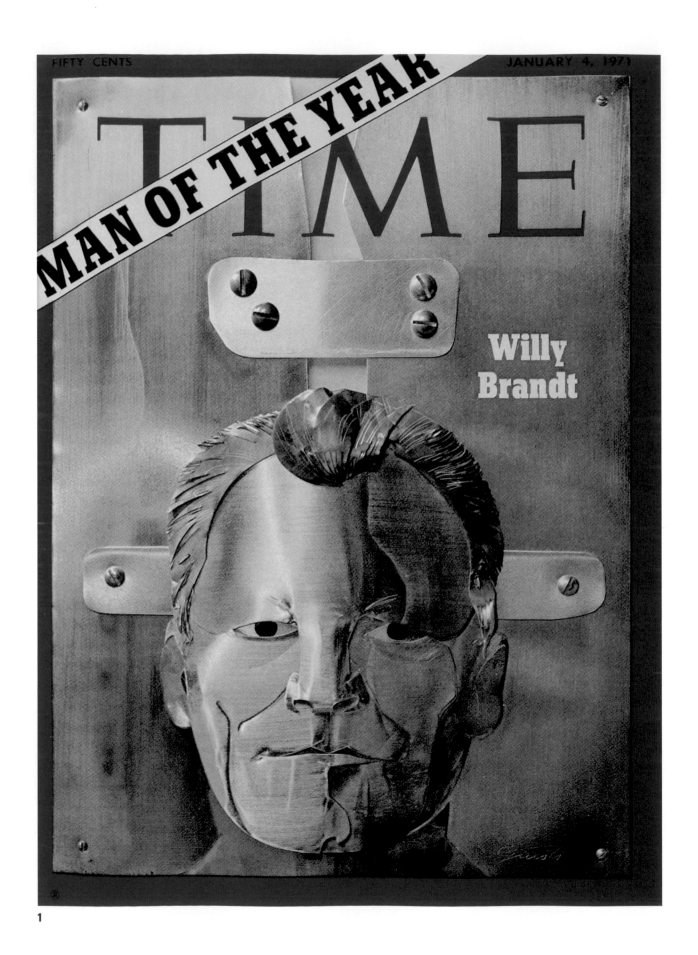

FIFTY CENTS   JANUARY 4, 1971

TIME

MAN OF THE YEAR

Willy Brandt

1

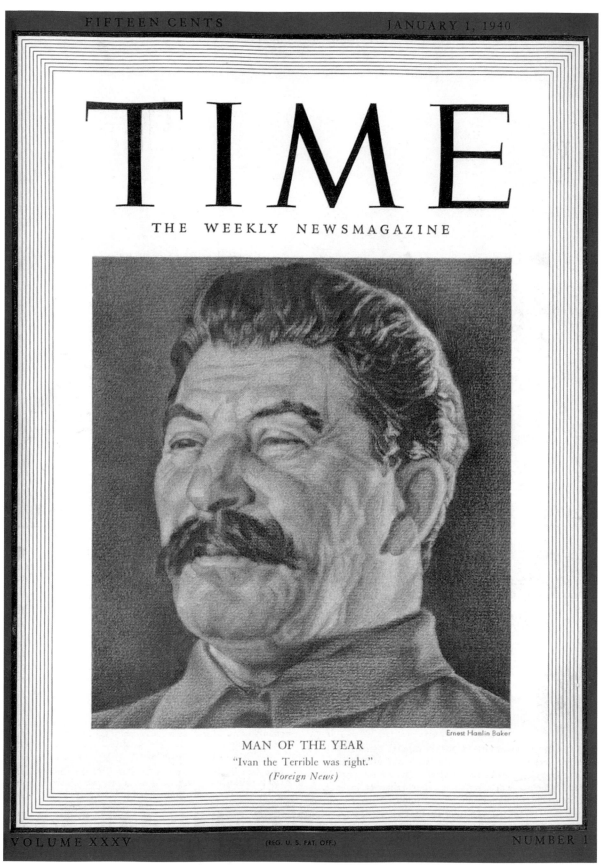

FIFTEEN CENTS   JANUARY 1, 1940

TIME

THE WEEKLY NEWSMAGAZINE

Ernest Hamlin Baker

MAN OF THE YEAR
"Ivan the Terrible was right."
(Foreign News)

VOLUME XXXV   (REG. U. S. PAT. OFF.)   NUMBER 1

2

3

4

The Art of Caricature

The birth of caricature as a form of independent expression can be traced to the end of the 16th century and the work of Bernini, Arcimboldo and the Carracci brothers. The physiognomy theories of the Swiss theologian Lavater (1741-1801), very much in vogue in the 16th century, had considerable influence on portraitists of the time. According to Lavater a person's physiognomy could reveal traits of their character. Caricature sought to expose the truth about its subject's character visually. By the end of the 19th century and the beginning of the 20th, caricature had become a key feature of the press, playing a similar role to that of the pamphlet. Easily accessible, amusing and condensed, it was widely appreciated by the public. A fearsome weapon when wielded astutely, it proved that the pen was indeed often mightier than the sword.

The French School

The heyday of French caricature started in 1831 with the famous series of portraits of Louis-Philippe transformed into a pear, as depicted by Philipon, editor of the journal *Le Charivari* – it was swiftly condemned. Apart from Daumier, the best-known caricaturist of the period, a host of others, including Pigal, Gavarni, Gustave Doré, Grandville, Bertall, Nadar, Cham, Henri Monnier, Travies, Edmond Morin, Gill and Grévin stripped characters bare in the pages of *L'Éclipse, L'Intransigeant, La Caricature, Le Rire, Le Courrier français* and *L'Assiette au beurre,* to name but a few. The much imitated Swiss artist Töpffer launched the vogue for telling stories in pictures in *Le Chat noir,* a true ancestor of the modern comic strip.

English Satire

From Hogarth (1697-1764) to Thomas Rowlandson (1756-1827), James Gillray (1757-1815) and George Cruikshank (1792-1878), English caricature has a long and noble tradition. The satirical magazine *Punch,* based on the French *Charivari,* was the ideal canvas for the biting wit of drawings by John Leech, John Tenniel, du Maurier and later, David Low, Victor Weisz (Vicky) and Osbert Lancaster.

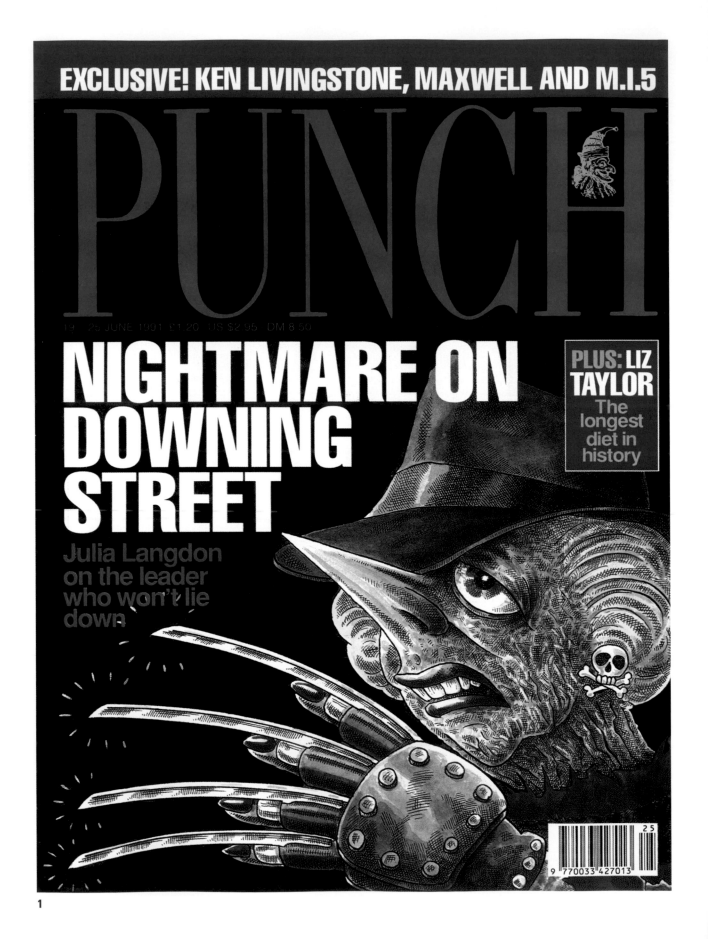

1

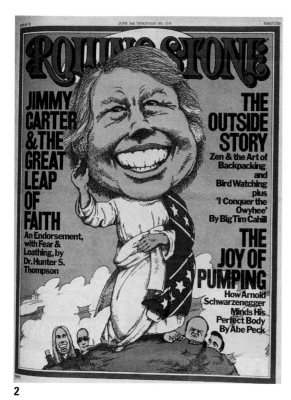

2

3

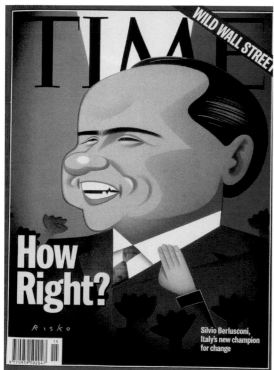

4

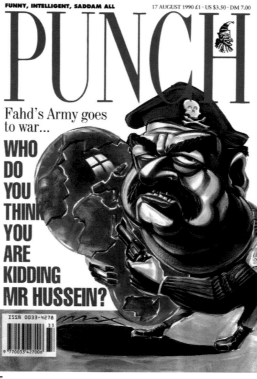

5

In the United States the first recognised caricaturist was Thomas Nast (1840-1902), whose work was published in *Harper's Weekly*. The genre bloomed in three main magazines: the pro-Democrat *Puck,* founded in 1877, the Republican *Judge* (1881-1937) and *Life* (1883-1935), with Charles Dana Gibson and Norman Rockwell.

Anti-Establishment

The Dreyfus affair which rocked France in 1894 created such debate that caricaturists joined the ranks of partisan newspapers and their warring opinions, with the 'for' camp including Forain and Caran d'Ache in *Psst* and the 'anti-Dreyfus' camp including Hermann Paul and Ibels in *Le Sifflet*. At the same time in Germany, the anti-establishment weekly *Simplicissimus,* founded in 1897, made satire, particularly of the illustrated kind, its expressive warhorse. The same satirical vein was mined in *The Caricatural Review,* founded in Russia in 1908 and which survived for all of thirteen days. From 1900 to 1918, Alsatian caricaturists were particularly militant: Hansi, Zislin, Robert Beltz, André Wenger, Roland Peuckert and above all Tomi Ungerer, who had an international career. The inter-war years were a fertile period for the last great generation of French caricaturists with Gassier in *Le Canard enchaîné* and Sennep in *Le Coup de patte*. A true institution in the satirical press was born in Russia in 1922: *Krokodil,* founded by Mikhaïl Tcheremnykh, Victor Deni and Ivan Milioutine, and which is still in print today. Its militant caricatures signed by one Koukriniksy were actually the work of three artists, Mikhaïl Kouprianov, Porfin Krilov and Nikolaï Sokolov. Although caricature found a new lease of life in England in the 1950s, with Ronald Searle, Gerald Scarfe and Ralph Steadman, it was a throwback to the aesthetics of the 19th century, particularly in the illustrations of the American David Levine, whose works first appeared in *New York Review of Books* in 1963.

1. *Punch.* Margaret Thatcher. 19th-25th June 1991. 2. *Rolling Stone.* Jimmy Carter. 3rd June 1976. 3. *Stern.* Leonid Brezhnev. Drawing by John Mulatier, 3rd May 1978. 4. *Time.* Silvio Berlusconi. Drawing by Robert Risko, 11th April 1994. 5. *Punch.* Saddam Hussein. 17th August 1990.

Artists and the Press

One might well consider Mehemed Fehmy Agha to be the first modern art director. Appointed Art Director of *Vogue* by Condé Nast in 1929, and of *Vanity Fair,* he fought for four-colour printing on the cover, frequently handing its illustration to artists. Forty years later the tradition continued when *Vogue* (2) hired Dalí, who doctored a photograph of Marilyn Monroe, giving her a hint of Mao Tse Tung, simultaneously paying homage to his wife Gala, the ideal woman, and Marilyn, the little 'mother' of the people. A painter and self-proclaimed genius, Dalí was at ease in all media: illustration and photomontage for the press, as well as advertising, jewellery and performance art. When Man-Ray took Dalí's illuminated portrait for the cover of *Time* (4) in 1934, he immortalised Dalí's 'critical-paranoia', and 'spontaneous method of irrational consciousness'.

Whether they contributed occasionally or were employed to produce a certain number of covers, many artists, painters, photographers and illustrators found another avenue

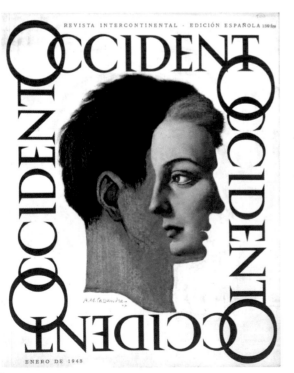

1. *Occident.* Cover, A. M. Cassandre. January 1948. 2. *Vogue. Dedicated to Gala,* drawing, Salvador Dalí. Marilyn Monroe. Photo, Philippe Halsman/Magnum, "Mao-ified" by Dalí, December-January 1971/1972. Art Directors, Jocelyn Kagère, Simone Hibon and Yves Goude. 3. *Esquire.* Cover, Jean-Paul Goude and Pierre Houles, September 1974. Art Director, Richard Weigand. 4. *Time.* Dalí by Man Ray, with the authorisation of James T. Soby, 14th December 1936. 5. *Life.* Photo, Henri Cartier-Bresson/Magnum, 13th February 1950. Art Director, Charles Tudor. 6. *Fortune.* Cover, Fernand Léger, December 1941. Art Director, Francis E. Brennan.

of expression in the press. The illustrator Cassandre, hired by Alexey Brodovitch to produce covers for *Harper's Bazaar* is a good example. Very well known for his talent as a poster artist – the famous Dubo, Dubon, Dubonnet triptych of 1932 was his work – and inventor of a number of stylish fonts, he attached particular importance to the relationship between the image and the typography. 'Each letter is part of the rhythm, like individual gestures of a choreographer. Each letter communicates this rhythm to a word, phrase, whole line and page,' he once commented. He proved his point in the cover that he produced for the magazine *Occident* in January 1948 (1).

Exercises in Decorative Art

Jean-Paul Goude, the illustrator, photographer, and director of commercials, was a fervent admirer of *Harper's Bazaar* and *Esquire*. He and his friend Jean Lagarrigue decided to send some of their work to two American magazines on the off chance they might get noticed. It worked and they became art directors of *Esquire* (3). Less surprising was Henri Cartier-Bresson's work on Indonesia for *Life*. A fearless and even-handed photojournalist, Cartier-Bresson had his first reportage published in 1932 by *Vu*, founded the Magnum agency with Robert Capa and other colleagues in 1947 and explored Indonesia with his camera after the country's independence.

Fortune and Léger

Fortune, the American business monthly that made technical news available to its readers, rightly prided itself on the excellence of its visuals, so it was only natural that it should call upon the talents of Fernand Léger in 1941 (6). Exiled in America, the painter from Normandy had followed Cézanne's instruction to 'treat nature by the cylinder, the sphere and the cone, putting it all into perspective', taking his inspiration from what he termed 'shop front art', that of industrial products, advertisements and luminous signs. This effective use of geometry practically leaps off the magazine's cover.

Off the Page

In heraldry mise-en-abîme consists of placing one blazon inside a second. In literature it is a narrative within a narrative, a technique that has been employed since Homer and that was revived in the early 20th century. Transposed into graphic design it is often referred to as the 'Vache Qui Rit' effect, in reference to the famous brand image of the French soft-cheese product, which shows a cow wearing earrings made of cheese wedges that each bear a label showing the same cow wearing the same earrings. This vertiginous effect confers a kind of three dimensional aspect to an image. In literature it often serves to increase the illusion of reality in a tale. If the narrator finds a manuscript that itself contains a narrative, then he or she immediately gains in credibility. The same is true of images. The illusory depth highlights the foreground, providing the foundation on which other themes, ideas or fantasies can be built.

Explosive Covers

The torn effect is frequently used for magazine covers, although it generally suggests not infinite repetition but a window on the world (2, 4, 6), an accurate description of the function of the press.

The basic effect is one of surprise, reminding us of acrobats diving circus-like through paper hoops (1, 3). There is the slightly disturbing feeling of something hitherto only suggested taking shape, made flesh, rushing from out of some obscure backdrop, like a toy doll bursting out of its wrapping (5). Then comes the violent explosion, the fiery gaze or shooting fist of characters who seek to break out of their paper prison (7, 9). In these examples the subjects seem to come alive, to move towards the reader, thereby reminding us of three effects magazines aim to procure: the pleasure of familiarity (hi! I'm your friend), take-home dreams (the clown, the star and the beauty brought alive just for us) and warning (we're on the lookout, but pay attention, things are happening).

While bringing events closer to the reader the tear or rip also packs a violent punch. War sets *Le Point* on fire (4), *Time* has its cover

1

2

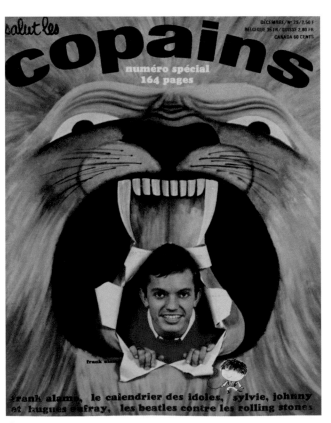

3

4

5

6

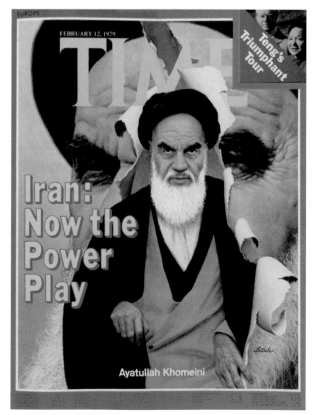

7

8

ripped as the Russian bear mauls Yeltsin (10), while as the Israeli-Arab conflict divides the Middle East, the cover of *Time* is also rent asunder (8). In each case a striking montage underlines a hot topic of the day. On closer inspection however, it is not so much the character depicted who comes to life, but the magazine that frames the event which gains in credibility. It has been roughed up and threatened, but remains indestructible. The clown's hat disappears under the reassuring label of the *Post* (1) that has been pinned over it, while the fighter jet that rips *Time* in two (8) will not reach the 'E' of the title. That is the nature of the news magazine, a genre that *Time* defined: stick to the facts, use pictures, but keep a certain objective distance.

1. *The Saturday Evening Post.* Cover, John Atherton, 8th July 1944. 2. *Le Figaro magazine.* Photo, Piquemal/Rapho, 7th August 1991. 3. *Salut les copains.* Photo, Jean-Marie Périer, drawing, Jean Alessandrini, December 1964. 4. *Le Point.* Cover, Bureau/Sygma, 2nd December 1974. Art Director, Philippe Charliat. 5. *Die Woche.* Photo, Yvan Dalain, 1st to 7th June 1953. 6. *Stern.* 7. *Time.* Photo, Lettick, 12th February 1979. Art Director, W. Bernard. 8. *Time.* Cover, Norman Gorbaty, 22nd June 1970. Art Director, Louis R. Glessmann.

Overleaf
9. *Newsweek.* Photo, Constantine Manos/Magnum, 17th April 1967. Art Director, Alfred Lowry. 10. *Time.* Photo-illustration, Dennis Chalkin. Yeltsin by Sergei Guneyev, 5th April 1993. Art Director, Rudolph C.Hoglund.

Newsweek

APRIL 17, 1967

THE DEFENDER

IN SHEPPARD TRIAL   Pleas Judge   Coppoli

Curb Actions at

New Witne

TRIAL SU

MURDER

Sheppard Fr

rangler Susp

Murder.

Witnes

ailey Accus

'RANGLER' JURY
GETS CASE TODAY

murder. He is on
series of lesser
related to the killin
burglary, robbery

ry Finds

NOT GUIL

JURY

polino. He also is charged
rder in the first degr
for the 1963 sla

ESTI. Y I

Bailey .

Defends

ot Guilty

BAILEY.

LIENT KILLED 1
AILEY TELLS JU

NT ACCUSED

JURY FI

SHEPP

olino   Acq

Defense Attor
F. Lee Bailey

APRIL 5, 1993 No. 14

TIME

INTERNATIONAL

... BUT UNBOWED

MITTERRAND: The Last Lap

9 770959 502023

14

A Short History of Art Directors

Ten mouths bursting onto the page, surprising effects of framing and contrast, sensuality, aggression and seduction, here in a nutshell is the history of the art director, a profession that was born in the United States in the 1920s, but whose leading lights hailed from Europe. Trained in the advertising industry, they soon claimed a foothold in the illustrated press.

Agha the Pioneer

Mehemed Fehmy Agha was probably the first true modern art director. The New York publisher Condé Nast brought him over from Berlin, where he had been working for German *Vogue,* and appointed him Art Director of *Vogue, House and Garden* and *Vanity Fair.* Agha invented a new way of working. He was the first to consider the magazine as a series of double pages rather than individual pages, introducing the use of double-page mock-ups prepared using fake text and extremely detailed collages instead of the customary pencil sketches. He planned an entire issue before commissioning photographers, composing the text in harmony with the images. His was an entirely new logic, centred fully on the magazine's visuals.

Alexey Brodovitch arrived from Paris to teach in Philadelphia in 1934, before becoming art director of *Harper's Bazaar,* where he hired the illustrator Cassandre to create numerous covers and trained a whole generation of artists. Among the émigrés who influenced

1. *Vogue.* Cover, Blumenfeld, January 1950. Art Director, Alexander Liberman. **2.** *City.* Cover, Jeff Manzetti, November 1986. Art Directors, Frédérique Courtadon and Guy-Alain Meyer. **3.** *Stern.* 1970. **4.** *Figaro magazine.* 31st October 1992. Art Director, Laurence Galud. **5.** *Jet Society.* Cover, Andy Warhol, Spring 1987. Art Director, Vicky Fabian. **6.** *Follow me.* Photo, Dossier and graphic design, Mike Yavel/Sipa Press, 26th December 1991. **7.** *Vogue.* May 1945.

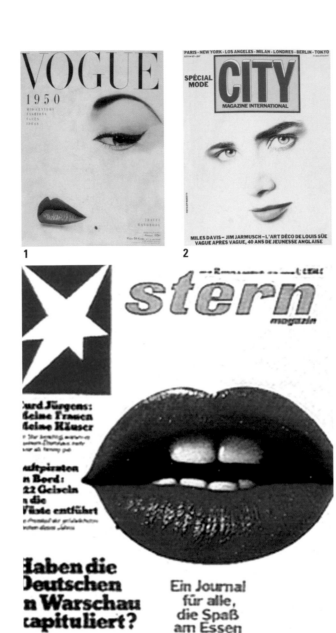

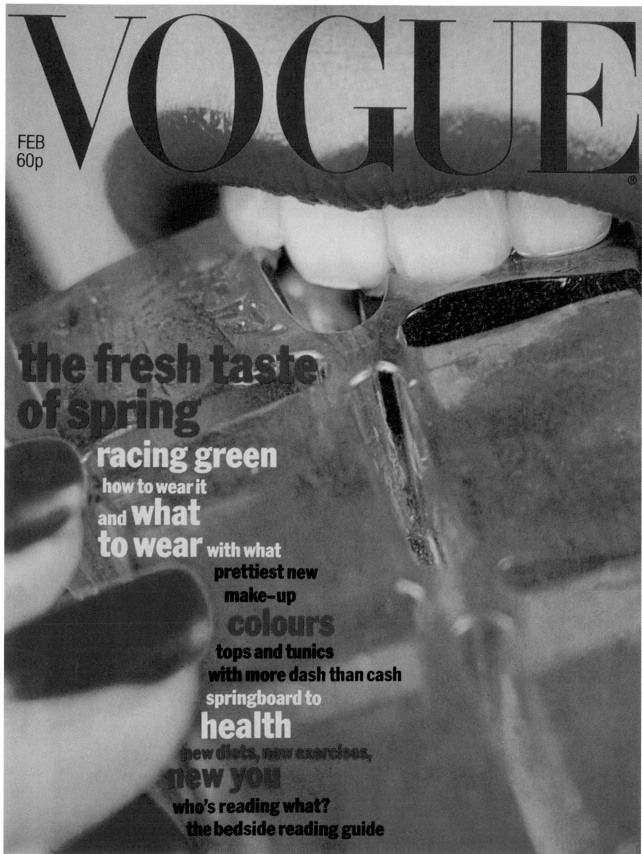

8

9

8. *Vogue.* Photo, Willie Christie, February 1977. Art Director, Terry Jones. 9. *Zoom.* Elisabeth photographed by Marc Robin, May 1976. Art Director, Maurice Coriat. 10. *Vogue Hommes.* Cover, Hans Feurer, Spring 1975. Art Directors, Jocelyn Kargère, Simone Hibon, Paul Wagner, Alexis Stoukoff and Guillaume Bruneau.

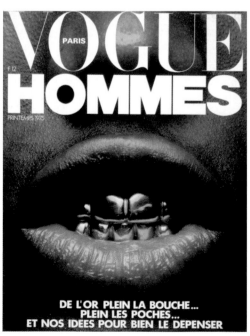

10

American graphic design were Will Burtin, art director of *Fortune* in the 1940s, Ladislav Sutnar, Herbert Bayer, Moholy-Nagy and Gyorgy Kepes.

Form and Content

At the same time, several American graphic designers were starting their careers, including the poster artist Lester Beall, art director of the pharmaceutical journal *Scope,* Alvin Lustig, who reinvented typography, Paul Rand, the collage wizard, art director of *Esquire* and *Apparel Arts* who also ran an advertising agency, and Herb Lubalin, a great conceptualist who was handed the responsibility in 1961 of giving *The Saturday Evening Post* a makeover. This primacy of concept created by Lubalin and borrowed by others, was particularly visible on the covers of *Esquire,* which successively employed two of the principal graphic artists of the 1950s, Henry Wolf, who succeeded in increasing sales of the magazine considerably, before leaving to join *Harper's Bazaar,* and George Lois, whose compositions relied upon the reader's ability to decipher the meaning of retouched images. But it was not until the middle of the 1960s that graphic design was finally recognised as a profession in its own right, with specialised monthlies such as *Print, Communication Arts* and *Art Direction.*

A Few Graphic Effects

The human face is by far the most frequently used graphic element on magazine covers. Once the eye has been caught all kinds of other elements can be added to destabilise the viewer. The obstructed gaze hidden behind binoculars and glasses (15 to 18) is one of advertising's strongest weapons. But the face can also become an object, as in the two covers representing targets: the head of Saddam Hussein is turned into a map targeted by the cross-hairs of a sniper rifle (11) and a silhouette on a shooting range (12). Finally, photomontage enables one to play with varying proportions (13, 16) that function as riddles. Graphic designers have truly invented a new language.

11

12

13

14

11. *La Revue du Liban.* 19th to 26th December 1998. **12.** *Time.* Cover, Wilson McLean, 3rd February 1992. Art Director, Rudolph C.Hoglund. **13.** *Le Point.* Cover, Yves Dejardin after *L'Expresso,* 6th December 1976. Art Director, Jacques Eyzat. **14.** *Stern.* Photo, Sylvain Corrodi, 13th June 1976.

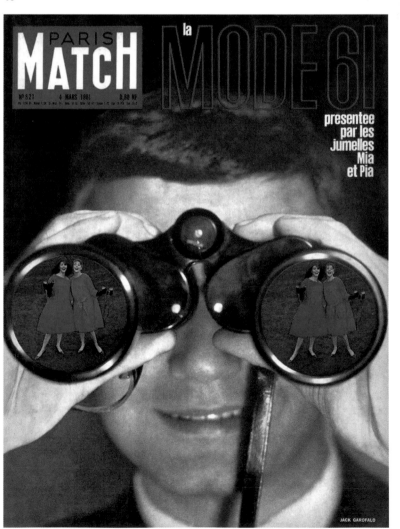

Chic, Trash and Fun

Kitsch is a German word that has no equivalent. It describes an aesthetic that encompasses objects or items of decoration labelled as tasteless by established culture. First appearing in Bavaria under the reign of Louis II, kitsch can be divided into three distinct periods: around 1900, at the time of the modern style; the styling of the 1930s; the pop art of the 1960s. Because of its fun factor, it had considerable influence on magazines as early as the 1930s, particularly on women's publications that wished to affirm the wild desires of effervescent good humour. It is an intensely optimistic art form, not only in terms of its frivolity, but also as a sort of call to gaiety, as characterised by the magazine *Marie-Claire* which was launched in 1939.

Cheese!

Kitsch and the magazine press might have been made for each other. Each serves to satisfy a burning desire for images, dreams and symbols, served up in a manner that is often gratuitous and crazily playful – from the little pig proudly shown off like a baby (4), the intimate tête à tête shared with a baby goat (3), the pouting mouth poised to bestow tender

Tricky, a woolly monkey, has been Miss West's pet for two years

1

2

3

4

1. **Life**. Photo, Philippe Halsmar 18th April 1969. Art Director, Bernar Quint. 2. **Quick**. 9th April 1955. 3 **Constanze**. Photo, Schmölcke, Apr 1954. 4. **Deutsche Illustrierte**. Photo Deutsch Cosmopolfilm, 4th Januar 1958. 5. **Cinémonde**. 29th March 1939 6. **Film Fun**. October 1940.

kisses on a pair of budgerigars (6) to the cherub-faced monkey sitting on a plinth against a Barbie-doll background (1), bucolic scenes of country beauties in doll-like poses (5), or droll whimsy (2). The outrageous euphoria frequently verges on the ridiculous, and it is always a breath of fresh air. Just as kitsch tames nature in improbable ways, women too break free from conventional shackles to play fantastical roles (satin-clad diva, parasol-bearing contessa, bowler-hatted tomboy, etc.) that are so grossly exaggerated that they can only provoke hilarity.

Too Much?

The advent of kitsch at the end of the 19th century was made possible through the industrialisation of art. Zinc was coated to look like bronze, leatherette made its appearance, as did colourful plastics, mass-produced porcelains and mouldings of papier-mâché, often using old, particularly baroque, motifs. From the 1930s to the 1960s, magazine culture also provided doses of this manufactured happiness. The readers could always tell the real from the fake. But humorous covers made them smile, and whether the joke was on the readers or on the magazine itself, it mattered little. People loved it.

5

6

The Art of Pop Culture

Pop art and pop music are essential aspects of the urban American culture of 1955-1960. But the term pop art actually originated in England, at a time when post-war Europe was busily importing the American way of life. The term describes the cross between art and this new society in which economic necessity and mass consumerism led to a standardisation of mass-produced manufactured goods and the proliferation of media, advertising and marketing techniques.

Many pop artists came from advertising and brought their techniques with them: simple, direct messages and images that could be endlessly reproduced; an impersonal touch and efficiency took priority over aesthetics. In Andy Warhol's view shopping malls were the new museums. The work of art was no longer necessarily a singular object. It might reproduce an image already seen in the media or advertising, as in Warhol's famous reproductions of cans of Campbell's Soup. But pop art was also more than a style; it was a state of mind best summarised by one of its pioneers, Richard Hamilton, who defined pop art as 'popular, transient, expendable, low-cost, mass-produced, young, witty, sexy, gimmicky, glamorous and very big business.'

Enduring Ephemera

Pop art was a rather scandalous success. Abstract expressionism was at its peak and yet here it was confronted with images that had been hitherto neglected, borrowed from advertising and comic strips. Was this a return to some sort of facile figurative vein? There were accusations of the intrusion of mercantilism into art. The shock came in 1964 when the prize of the Venice Biennale was awarded to Rauschenberg. A form that had never really considered itself as a movement now received international acclaim.

It was initially considered a passing fad, soon to be discarded and forgotten, just like the themes it depicted and the materials it used. Yet today we are forced to recognise that the pop aesthetic marked a turning point in the history of modern art. And despite the intel-

1

2

3

4

lectual scorn heaped upon the pop artists themselves, they were behind many of the artistic developments of the 1970s and 1980s. Perhaps the most popular and certainly the most high profile of these artists was Andy Warhol. His death in 1987 made headlines, for his style had inspired the covers of countless magazines for twenty years. According to Roy Lichtenstein nearly everyone had a bit of pop in them. Pop art no longer shocks. It has become a part of the language of art.

The Work

Roy Lichtenstein borrowed the pictorial style of popular American comic strips: garish colours and industrial printing processes proudly vaunting their pixels, as seen in the cover of *Newsweek* (3). Similar comic strip influences are evident on the cover of *Actuel* (1) and turned up in the graphic designs of many other magazines and journals. Still, Lichtenstein was voted 'the worst painter of the year' by *Vogue,* an example of the ambiguous nature of pop art, considering that Andy Warhol himself had started his career as an advertising artist for the very same magazine. The star system, an essential element of the American Way of Life, was one of the preferred targets of pop art and no icon was too sacred, from Marilyn Monroe, star of the silver screen, to the Coca-Cola bottle, veritable emblem of the consumer society, as well as political personalities from Mao to François Mitterrand, as depicted by Andy Warhol on the cover of *Le Nouvel Observateur* (4) in 1982, twenty years after pop art first burst onto the scene.

1. *Actuel.* Illustration taken from Super Mädchen by Meysenburg, January 1971. **2.** *Friends.* 5th April 1971. **3.** *Newsweek.* Cover, Roy Lichtenstein, 25th April 1966. Art Director, Alfred Lowry. **4.** *Le Nouvel Observateur.* Cover, Andy Warhol, 8th to 14th May 1982.

Snapshots of Everyday America

'There are two artists in the United States whom every American knows, whether they be black or white, rich or poor, art-lover or illiterate. They are Walt Disney and Norman Rockwell.' This was how *Time* magazine paid homage to Rockwell after his death in 1978 at the age of 84. The two thousand paintings that he left behind constitute a true pictorial history of an era and a people, sketched from the most authentic scenes of everyday life, not just how life was, but how one might wish it to be.

Slices of Life

Born in New York in 1894, Rockwell started painting as soon as he could hold a brush, receiving his first commission when he was only fifteen. He joined the National Academy School, which he found too strait laced, followed by the brand new Art Students League, where he met two of his masters, George Bridgeman and Thomas Fogarty. He was a fervent admirer of illustrators who were in vogue, like N. C. Wyeth, Howard Pyle (collecting and examining all of the journals that published his work) and particularly J. C. Leyendecker. When Rockwell was still a teenager he was already known in the youth magazines, with many of his illustrations published in *Boys' Life,* the Scout magazine, of which he very soon became the editor. He also worked on the weeklies *Colliers, Leslie's* and *Judge,* then on *Life, Literary Digest* and *Country Gentleman.* At 19, they were already calling him the 'boy illustrator', his first taste of celebrity. In 1916 he travelled to Philadelphia to meet George Horace Lorimer, the editor of *The Saturday Evening Post,* who commissioned two paintings from him for the cover. This now meant he had an audience of two million people and marked the beginning of an adventure that would last 47 years.

American Society in Every Detail

Until 1919, four-colour printing was rare, owing to its expense. Rockwell's first pictures were in black and white, like those of Howard Pyle, then red was added. He worked in oil. Half of the covers that he produced for *The*

1

2

3

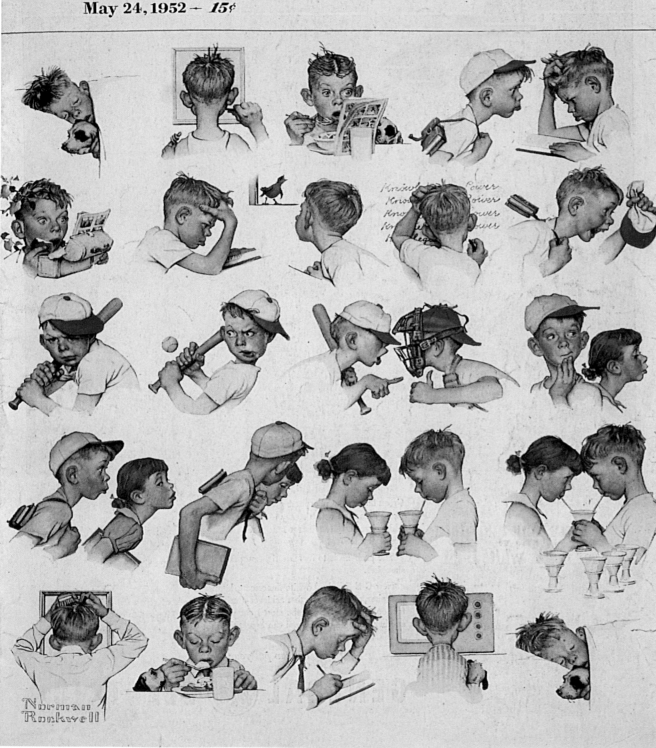

Saturday Evening Post depicted children or teenagers, like the one of 'Cousin Reginald', showing tidy little boys, as well as playground scenes or the unforgettable medical check-up. From 1919, Rockwell started to depict adults as well, preferably in scenes of family life in an idealised small town America, but always with a touch of humour. Presidents Eisenhower, Kennedy and Johnson, as well as Nasser and Nehru all had their portraits painted by him for the covers of *The Saturday Evening Post*.

From War to Peace

During the Second World War, Rockwell painted thirty-three covers, depicting the war from the viewpoint of civilians. A third of these pictures were devoted to the fictitious character of Willie Gillis, 'the most famous American soldier', although he was never shown on the field of battle. In 1943 Rockwell published his depiction of the 'four essential liberties of man' in *The Post,* inspired by Roosevelt's speech. The paintings toured the country to help sell war bonds. Celebrity soon followed and Rockwell was feted as *the* American painter, or at least illustrator, since recognition from the artistic milieu was not quite as forthcoming as that of the general public.

In the 1950s living models were replaced by photographs, which were cheaper. Rockwell saw this change as a betrayal of the rules of art, but his work continued to gain in precision. By 1963 he had painted 324 covers for *The Saturday Evening Post* when the magazine decided to stop publishing illustrations on the cover. Rockwell subsequently went to work for *Look* for ten years, then *McCall's*.

1. *The Saturday Evening Post.* 24th November 1945. **2.** *Life.* 10th April 1919. **3.** *The Satuday Evening Post.* 26th May 1945. **4.** *The Saturday Evening Post.* 24th May 1952. Art Director, Kenneth Stuart.

Art in the Interwar Years

The term Art Deco comes from the 'Exposition Internationale des Arts Décoratifs et Industriels Modernes' that was held in Paris in 1925. The movement was a reaction to the excesses of the Art Nouveau of the 1900s, whose frills were derided as 'noodle style'. Art Deco marked the reappearance of rigour and a distillation of forms, influenced by the clean classical lines of Greco-Roman styles and the geometric lines of Egyptian architecture, with vivid colours drawn from cubism and fauvism.

The Roaring Twenties

Art Deco met with success in the Roaring Twenties that followed the turmoil of the Great War, and showed a desire to return to traditional values in a climate of euphoria. The characteristic forms of Art Deco may be found in architecture, furniture and fashion. Although its exponents (like those of its contemporary, the German Bauhaus movement) dreamed of using industrial techniques for mass production, the style remained elitist. The angular precision and recessed contours of the style did not lend themselves to industrial processes. These objectives of Art Deco would only be realised with the popularity of the Streamline style in the 1930s and 1940s.

Text before Image

Art Deco painting remained on the margins of contemporary movements such as Cubism, Surrealism or Futurism. Its main thrust was decorative. Yet this style invaded the advertising, posters and press of the period. One of its main characteristics was the emphasis of letter and text in relation to the image, hence the particular care given to typography (2). With women as one of its subjects of predilection, Art Deco initially worked its way into the illustrations of fashion artists working on luxury magazines. These publications crossed the Atlantic to America where the Art Deco style found new homes in magazines such as

1. *Vogue.* February 1931. 2. *L'Officiel.* Illustration, P. A. Covillot, October 1934. 3.. *La Rivista.* Illustration, Amaldi, July 1928.

1

Vogue and *Harper's Bazaar*. Art Deco declined during the Thirties before the rise of Modernism and International Style, but its spirit lingered on in the imposing architecture of European totalitarianism in Germany, Italy and the USSR. The increasing heaviness of its geometrical shapes and overwhelming monumental weightiness were supremely representative of these regimes and their ideals.

3

Press and Propaganda – Dangerous Liaisons

The interwar years saw the rise and confrontation of two forms of totalitarianism, Communism and Fascism. Despite their apparent antagonism, these two movements established similarly systematic forms of propaganda in all aspects of society. They featured heavy use of symbols, designated scapegoats, employed ideological brainwashing to form a 'healthy' brigaded youth, and denounced cabals and conspiracies. Democratic parties were hard pressed to match them, for their own propaganda and publications paled in comparison to the simple yet powerful ideas of their adversaries.

Fascism versus Communism

During the German occupation of France, the only publications available to democrats and communists were clandestinely printed leaflets; these would become famous, with names like *Combat* or *Libération*. The established press was either shut down or collaborated. All publications became vectors of often subtly different propaganda. There was purely German propaganda, Vichyist propaganda glorifying Marshal Pétain and the anti-Semitic propaganda of the Far Right. All three coexisted in the same sphere but their individual objectives were quite different.

While the hammer and sickle motif of the Communists and French tricolour of the Right were strong, easily identifiable symbols, the same could not be said for the Socialists. The German Social Democrats had taken to striking out the Nazi swastika with their own triple arrow symbol. Advocated by a refugee in France after Hitler's victory, this symbol was adopted by the French Socialists in 1934 (2). Opposition to the Popular Front was symbolised by 'the 200 families' that became a label used recurrently in the left-wing press to designate the enemy. The incarnation of a scapegoat reached its peak with the explosion of anti-Semitic hatred. The cover of *Je vous hais* perfectly reflects its content (3) depicting everything that the far right detested: Léon Blum, both a Jew and leader of the Popular Front, towering over the Chamber of Deputies.

1

2

3

4

fraternité

GRAND DOCUMENTAIRE MENSUEL ILLUSTRÉ

JANVIER 1938 Nº 23

1 fr. 50

Complot
contre la France

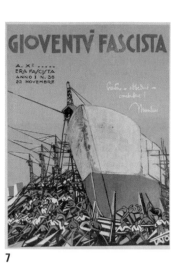

6

7

8

1. *Die Woche.* 30th October 1935. **2.** *Le Témoin.* 29th April 1934. **3.** *Je vous hais.* 17th April 1944. **4.** *Lafayette nous voici!* February 1943. **5.** *Fraternité.* January 1938. **6** *Crapouillot.* October 1933. **7.** *Gioventù Fascista.* Cover, Tato, 22nd November, year 1 of the Fascist era (1922). **8.** *Signal.* 1st June 1940.

Some propagandist publications of the Axis powers were of the highest quality. In Italy, graphic quality, often inspired by futurism, was unsurpassed (7), while in Germany photography reigned supreme (8). The magazine *Signal* was published in 8 languages across occupied Europe.

Conspiracy theories always provide the bedrock for extremists. The 'Conspiracy against France' announced on the cover of *Fraternité* (5) might well refer to a communist or Jewish conspiracy if it was a journal of the far right. But it is a communist magazine, and the conspiracy in this instance was fascist.

A Vichyist publication, *Lafayette nous voici!* (4) adroitly denounces American imposture, with the skeleton reaching out from its hiding place under the Statue of Liberty and the American flag to snatch France's North African colonies.

Unpredictable War

One of the paradoxes of wars is their unpredictable nature. Experts had agreed that the 1914-1918 war would last no longer than six months; nobody imagined that the Vietnam War would be won by what was thought of as the weaker side. The press related these false impressions, which were shared by the high command.

False Alarms

When war began to threaten Europe in 1936, magazine covers reflected two obsessive fears, poison gas attacks and air raids. Only the censored German press refused to worry about the upcoming conflict, with celebration of militarism the order of the day. The most horrific innovation of the Great War had been the use of poison gas. So it was generally thought that any future conflict would certainly see the widespread use of such munitions, both on soldiers and civilians. Photographs from the so called phony war show civilians calmly walking through the streets of Paris and London with their gas masks slung over their shoulders. But contrary to predictions, poison gas was never used during the Second World War in military operations in Europe. However, millions of Jews and others including gypsies and those classed as political or social undesirables were gassed by the Nazis in their concentration camps.

And Bombing?

The threat from the air and aerial bombardment was another cause of concern in the French and British press of the period. After all, in April 1937, Germany's Condor Legion had undertaken what may well have been the first ever deliberate aerial bombardment of a civilian target, when it attacked Guernica in Northern Spain, a bastion against Franco's army, killing more than 1,500 people and wounding hundreds more. France's swift defeat in 1940 meant that they escaped massive aerial bombardment. Britain was not so fortunate. Between September 7th 1940 and May 1941, massive German bombing raids on London and other major cities killed over 40,000 and left 1.4 million people homeless. But Britain's retaliation was even more terrible,

1

with 300,000 German civilians killed and 800,000 wounded in allied bombing raids. Although Bomber Command's argument for their blitz of German cities was that it would shorten the war and save many allied lives, bombing did little to dent Germany's arms production, except towards the end of the war when targeting was switched away from what was left of German cities to German industry and infrastructure. New fears would arise with the dawn of the nuclear age in 1945.

1. *Notre combat.* January 1944. 2. *I.R.Z.* Illustration, E. Deul, 23rd January 1932. 3. *Voilà.* 19th March 1937.

Overleaf
4. *Vu.* 17th April 1935. 5. *Vu.* 22nd March 1933. 6. *Vu.* Cover, N.YT., 13th December 1933. 7. *Vu Lu.* 21st March 1936. 8. *Vu.* 29th March 1933. 9. *Vu.* 24th April 1935. 10. *Vu.* 11th February 1931.

VU

PRÉDICTION DES ASTRES

1935,
PAS DE GUERRE

PAR
MAURICE
PRIVAT

DANS CE NUMÉRO :

STRESA
PAR J. SAUERWEIN

8e ANNÉE. — N° 370
17 AVRIL 1935
PRIX : 2 FRANCS
Directeur : Lucien VOGEL
PARAIT LE MERCREDI

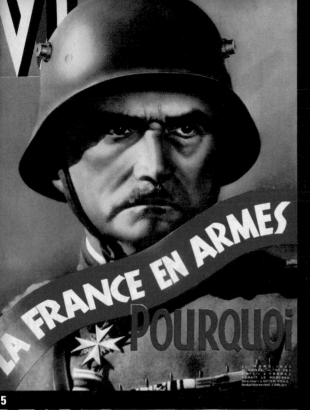

VU

L'ALLEMAGNE EN ARMES

COMMENT

VU

LA FRANCE EN ARMES

POURQUOI

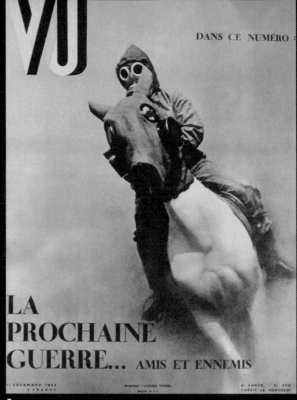

VU

DANS CE NUMÉRO :

LA PROCHAINE GUERRE... AMIS ET ENNEMIS

VU

NUMÉRO SPÉCIAL

DE NOUVEAU LE SPECTRE DE LA GUERRE

UNE DOCUMENTATION IMPRESSIONNANTE

26 PAYS DÉVOILENT LE SECRET DE LEUR FORCE ET LA FRANCE ?

PRIX : 4 FRANCS
NUMÉRO SPÉCIAL
SAMEDI 21 MARS 1936
Directeur : Lucien VOGEL

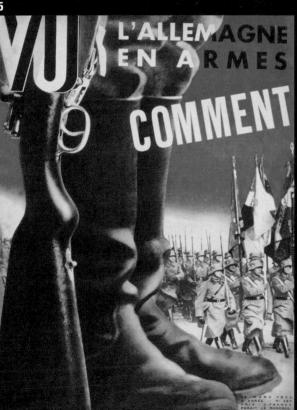

VU

MENACE AÉRIENNE ALLEMANDE

PRIX : 2 FR.

VU

NUMÉRO SPÉCIAL

LA PROCHAINE GUERRE

PARAIT LE MERCREDI
11 FÉVRIER 193
PRIX : 4 FRANC

5

6

7

8

9

10

The Second World War as Seen by *Life* – Men at Arms

When the United States entered the war in December 1941 it had already been raging for two years in Europe. During the 1920s and 1930s the vast majority of Americans supported their country's isolationist policies of staying neutral and letting the incorrigible Europeans sort out their own squabbles. Despite Roosevelt's personal support of Britain and America's financial and economic assistance, Congress, supported by public opinion and the press, had not the slightest intention of being dragged into the conflict. Opinion made a sharp U-turn after the Japanese attack on Pearl Harbor. Enraged by this act of aggression, the American people and government set their goal: the unconditional surrender of the enemy, whatever the means.

War, American-Style

The America of 1941 did not have a large army and had only recently started to equip it properly. Civilian and industrial contribution was therefore essential to the war effort. Almost overnight, car manufacturers found themselves designing and producing tanks, while America's commercial and technological know-how switched to the logistics of sending men and material halfway across the world. For many GIs this was the first time they had left their own state, let alone their country, and the Coca-Cola company did its very best to ensure that its taste of home was supplied to the front line. Press coverage of the war was also unprecedented. While this provided an excellent platform for propaganda and morale-boosting, it also revealed the workings of the military much more than ever before. When General Patton, one of the army's best tacticians, reportedly slapped a shell-shocked soldier, accusing him of cowardice, the press led a campaign against him that obliged Eisenhower to demand a public apology from Patton. The press were determined to follow all military operations and publicly denounced the lack of organisation surrounding them. In a country that had never known official state censorship, restrictions were limited only to military opera-

LIFE

APRIL 9, 1945   **10** CENTS
YEARLY SUBSCRIPTION $4.50

1

LIFE
SOVIET SOLDIER
FEBRUARY 12, 1945 **10** CENTS
YEARLY SUBSCRIPTION $4.50

2

LIFE
PANAMA DEFENSE
MARCH 17, 1941 **10** CENTS
YEARLY SUBSCRIPTION $4.50

3

LIFE
ARMY AIR OBSERVER
FEBRUARY 22, 1943 **10** CENTS
YEARLY SUBSCR.

4

LIFE
UNS FOR MERCHANTMEN
FEBRUARY 23, 1942 **10** CENTS
YEARLY SUBSCRIPTION $4.50

5

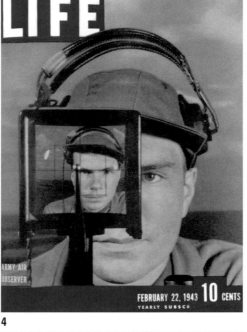

LIFE
INVADER
MAY 27, 1940 **10** CENTS

6

LIFE
DEFENSE ISSUE
U.S. ARMS
JULY 7 1941 **10** CENTS

7

tions that required top secrecy. Journalists' self-censorship did the rest.

Like many other magazines *Life* conveyed another essential aspect of this war: America's belief, still as strong today if not stronger, that quantitative and qualitative superiority of arms was essential to crush the enemy and spare soldiers' lives. The mass conversion of industry to arms production meant that by 1943 total American arms production surpassed that of all the other aggressors. The press paid particular attention to the work of women, called up to work in factories to replace men who had been drafted; they produced everything from artillery shells to bombers. But the main focus was of course on the men themselves and their material, from stock-piling of weaponry (5), to impressive artillery pieces (3) and sophisticated technology (4). We also see men armed and ready (2, 7), though not necessarily in action since it was not thought to be good for morale.

Fear of Casualties

The *Life* cover photograph of 9th April 1945 (1) is a rare exception. It shows marines under fire during the battle for Iwo Jima, one of the bloodiest of the war. It also provided the most famous photo from the Pacific theatre: a group of marines raising the star spangled banner on the island's summit. Taking heavy casualties and confronted with an enemy that grew ever more desperate as the Allies closed in on Japan, the press speculated with horror on the American losses that an invasion of Japan might incur. Shortly afterwards, President Truman authorised the use of the atom bomb to force Japan to surrender, using the thousands of American lives saved to defend his decision. Technology had the last word, and the same principle is still a consideration in modern military strategy, and has marked the world's collective unconscious.

1. *Life.* Photo, W. Eugene Smith, 9th April 1945. 2. *Life.* Photo, P.I., 12th February 1945. 3. *Life.* Photo, Robert Yarnall Richie, 17th March 1941. Art Directors, Peter Piening and Worthen Paxton. 4. *Life.* Photo, Dmitri Kessel, 22nd February 1943. Art Director, Worthen Paxton. 5. *Life.* Photo, Eliot Elisofon, 7th July 1941. Art Directors, Peter Piening and Worthen Paxton. 6. *Life.* 27th May 1940. Art Directors, Peter Piening and Worthen Paxton. 7. *Life.* Photo, George Strock, 23rd February 1942. Art Director, Worthen Paxton.

The Vietnam War as seen by *Life* – Blood, Sweat and Tears

Lying between the two extremes of the Second World War and the Gulf War, the Vietnam War presents two essential characteristics: it was a war fought without consensus and without censorship. The life or death struggle between democracy and Nazi barbarism during the Second World War was clearly a just cause, but free press coverage was relatively limited, mainly for logistical and technological reasons. While the war against Iraq was perhaps not quite as justifiable as WWII – after all the US had previously backed and armed Saddam Hussein against Iran – it was intensively planned, both militarily and media-wise, by the Pentagon. Indeed journalists were presented with a smorgasbord of media resources, carefully collected and fed to them. For the lessons of Vietnam continued to haunt the corridors of the Pentagon: keep casualties to a minimum, maintain a high level of morale and tightly control access to information.

The strength of television is what shaped perception of the conflict in Vietnam. For ten years, between 1963 and 1973, it beamed the madness of combat, the wounded, the dying and the pain and misfortune of the civilian population into the heart of every American home. It provoked fierce debate concerning both the justification for involvement in Vietnam in the first place and the reasons for staying there.

Undermined

While television undermined the public's confidence in the war, photojournalism harried its conscience. In Vietnam, war reporters suffered alongside the soldiers. 135 of them were killed during the wars in Indochina and Vietnam. But their photographs related the intense experience of soldiers and civilians caught up in the thick of conflict. Although the rough edges of television reportages could be smoothed away in the editing room before broadcast, photographs were published precisely because of their shock factor. The famous photograph of the chief of the Saigon police killing a Vietcong prisoner with a bullet to the head was a blow to the image of America's

1

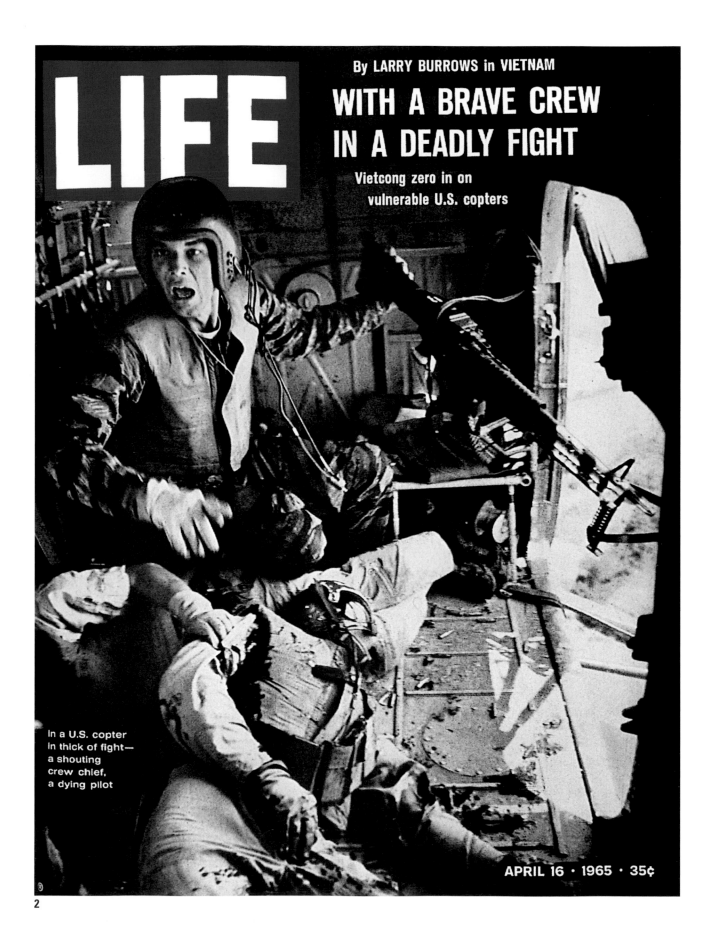

By LARRY BURROWS in VIETNAM

LIFE

WITH A BRAVE CREW IN A DEADLY FIGHT

Vietcong zero in on vulnerable U.S. copters

In a U.S. copter in thick of fight— a shouting crew chief, a dying pilot

APRIL 16 · 1965 · 35¢

South Vietnamese allies. That of a little naked girl fleeing a napalm attack went round the world. The two covers of *Life* shown here reveal a growing lassitude with the war.

Reversal of Opinion

The first cover is from 1966. Two ragged GIs, both with head wounds, seem abandoned in their trench. 'The war goes on', reads the caption. But for how long? And why? The public was starting to wonder. The second cover is from 1965, at the start of the war. It shows a helicopter evacuating a wounded pilot but it is evidently under attack. The realisation is dawning that the war might well be harder than first thought but victory still lies on the horizon. For the high command the solution lay with increasing the number of troops. They finally succeeded in getting conscription reintroduced and more than 500,000 men on the field. 1967 marked the start of the huge demonstrations against the draft. Liberal American youths and students had no wish to go and fight a war they felt did not concern them. The photograph of a young woman putting a flower in the barrel of a National Guardsman's rifle has also become legendary.

Good Guys and Bad Guys

The line between the good guys and the bad guys had become blurred. No matter that the North Vietnamese regime and their Vietcong guerrillas were responsible for much of the bloodshed and misery amongst their own population, it was time for the US to get out of this quagmire that had caused more than a million deaths, including those of 55,000 Americans. The last images of the Vietnam War show the chaotic evacuation of the American embassy in Saigon and the helicopters being pushed into the sea from the decks of the overloaded aircraft carriers. Freedom of the press is priceless. The Vietnam War proved how important it was in changing public opinion all round the world.

1. *Life.* Photo, Henri Huet/AP, 11th February 1966. Art Direction, Bernard Quint. **2.** *Life.* Photo, Larry Burrows, 16th April 1965. Art Direction, Bernard Quint.

2

Perfect Partners

The first fashion magazines appeared at the end of the 18th century and were a great success, thanks to their beautiful engravings. Their numbers increased over the course of the 19th century, and their pages were graced by the work of talented illustrators such as Carle Vernet in France. Prices rose as first colour plates were added, then, from 1880, patterns. The first magazine to reproduce a fashion photograph, and in what was only its second issue, was the French publication *La Mode Pratique* in 1891. The models became stars, particularly Mistinguett in the Parisian magazine *Les Modes.* Certain couturiers persisted however in maintaining the traditional aesthetics of the drawing. This enabled them to show their designs on bodies that were unnaturally slim, with perfect hour-glass figures and wonderfully long legs. Poiret had two albums published, in 1907 and 1908, that were drawn by Paul Iribe and Georges Lepape. Their aesthetics were reproduced by various luxury magazines like *Journal des Dames et des Modes,* which continued to appear until the Great War, *Gazette du Bon Ton* (1912-1925), edited by Lucien Vogel, and *Art, Goût et Beauté* (1920-1935).

Rendezvous with Elegance

Photography firmly established itself after the war, particularly in the American magazine *Vogue* that had just appeared in Europe. Along with the *Officiel de la couture* and *Harper's Bazaar* it was one of the three great fashion magazines, for which photographers such as Edward Steichen, Horst, Cecil Beaton, André Durot and the Baron de Meyer worked. New collections were presented in March and October, ballroom dresses and outfits in January, wedding dresses in May and hunting gear in September. But besides these society magazines, other less luxurious magazines were developing, aimed at a family clientele who wanted dress patterns and embroidery models. These included *Le Petit Écho de la Mode,* launched in 1880, *Modes et Travaux,* launched in 1919 and *Le Jardin des Modes,* launched in 1923.

In 1933, Carmel Snow from *Harper's Bazaar* hired a reporter to be a fashion photographer

1

2

3

4

and thereby created a new style of fashion photography. Exit studio shots of posed models and enter supposedly stolen pictures of working women in everyday, often outdoor settings. Photographers like Schall, O'Mearson and Moral took over. In 1937 Jean Prouvost launched *Marie-Claire,* a real novelty. Not only was it a magazine that was not devoted exclusively to fashion, but the elegant high society women were replaced by stars of the stage and screen, young, gay, charming women. In 1945 Hélène Lazareff took her inspiration from American publications to launch *Elle,* which she aimed at working women, not society matrons, and even succeeded in attracting male readers. With Christian Dior's *New Look,* femininity reigned supreme once more after the privations of the war. The American pin-up was triumphant

1. *ABC.* 17th April 1932. **2.** *Adam.* Cover, Garretto, 15th September 1936. **3.** *Hommes Magazine.* Cover, Robert Chauchy C., November 1971. **4.** *Cosmopolitan.* Cover, Coby Whitmore, May 1949. Art Director, Frank Eltonhead. **5.** *Paris toujours.* 31st January 1942. **6.** *The Sunday Times Magazine.* 28th August 1968.

and haute couture was now also aimed at very young women. This was when professional models started to replace actresses. These cover-girls, as they were called, were chosen from couture houses' most photogenic models. The most famous model of the 1950s was Bettina.

Era of the Ephemeral

In the 1960s, a new kind of fashion magazine appeared, designed for retailers. These publications reintroduced drawn models as opposed to photographed ones, giving them a more professional aspect. Inspired by these trade publications, some magazines read by the general public then adopted the use of sketches, too, so as to appear more professional when the new collections were launched. But while haute couture continued to fascinate, there was also a strong expansion in ready-to-wear. An article of clothing became an ephemeral consumer product, something that would have been unthinkable ten years prior. The ever younger models, wearing jeans and miniskirts, embodied casualness. The era was defined by Twiggy, with her androgynous adolescent body.

The Body Beautiful

Clothes became increasingly flashy and sexy with ever more flesh being shown. Another taboo was lifted: the bathroom and personal grooming. The women's press now devoted entire features to the decoration and arrangement of these private spaces, while there was a gradual fusion of the notions of fashion, beauty, health, hygiene, youth, sport and sexuality. Designers found themselves liberated by new textiles; their low cost brought fashion within reach of everyday women, an ever increasing number of whom were now not only working but creating fashion themselves. With the street now influencing haute couture, fashion magazines were now obliged to detect trends rather than seeking to create them.

1

2

3

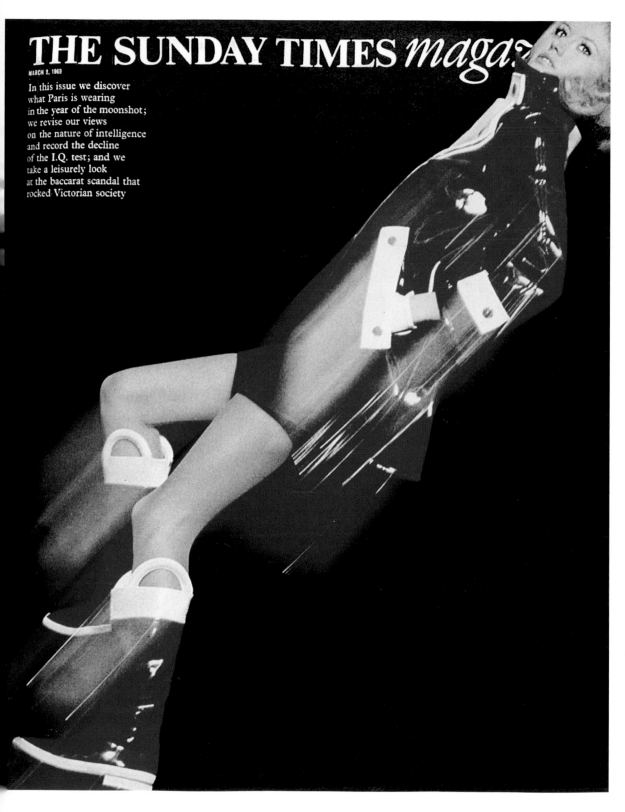

THE SUNDAY TIMES *maga*

MARCH 2, 1969

In this issue we discover
what Paris is wearing
in the year of the moonshot;
we revise our views
on the nature of intelligence
and record the decline
of the I.Q. test; and we
take a leisurely look
at the baccarat scandal that
rocked Victorian society

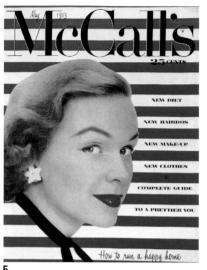

5

6

7

8

1. *L'Officiel.* December 1966. **2.** *Münchner Illustrierte.* 18th June 1955. **3.** *Ihre Freundin.* Photo, Fred Brommet/Rapho, January 1952. **4.** *The Sunday Times Magazine.* 2nd March 1969. **5.** *McCall's.* Cover, Leombruno-Bodi, May 1953. Art Director, John English. **6.** *Companion.* Cover, Topix, March 1955. Art Director, George W. Finnegan. **7.** *Album Figaro.* Cover, Henry Clarke, February-March 1950. **8.** *Kristall.* Cover, Sybille Oosterman, 4th quarter 1963. Art Directors, L. Bandelow, Wolfgang Dorn, Jochen Specht.

Transport of Dreams

Faster and further has always been one of man's eternal dreams. The invention of the steam engine by the Englishman George Stephenson in 1825 and the development of the rail-way network ushered in the greatest transport revolution since the invention of the wheel. In 1850 there were over 20,000 miles of railway line throughout the world. By 1914 the figure was over half a million.

The next revolution followed closely with the spread of electricity and the discovery of crude oil around 1860 in the United States and Russia. This latter industry grew dramatically with the development of the internal combustion engine and the creation of the automobile. It also heralded a cultural revolution. At a time when escape from the collective life of a family or community was still a fantasy, an individual or family vehicle offered freedom and speed for those able to afford it.

The first Paris Automobile Fair took place in 1898. By 1910 there were two million cars throughout the world.

From 1910 to 1970 the railway continued to make inroads in Latin America and Asia, but its star was waning in the older industrialised countries. The car became the symbol of the new consumer society. Until 1960 American

1

2

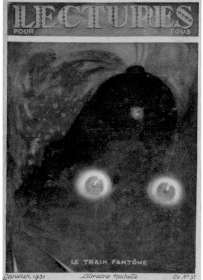

car production was as large as all other countries put together. In the United States the car had long been considered to be a working vehicle while in Europe it was still a luxury. Then when war-battered Europe got back on its feet again and wealth began to flow once more, this changed, and from the 1960s onwards in Europe the car became a family and then an individual object, mirroring the development of a lifestyle that had commenced in America in the 1920s.

Aesthetics of the Machine

Means of transport have inspired numerous artists and illustrators. Cubism, which had been derided by many art critics and the general public, found a new lease of life through artists such as Cassandre, Charles Loupot, Paul Colin and Carlu in France, McKnight-Kauffer and Ashley Avinden in the United States and Britain, and Biró in Hungary, through their work for advertising and poster art (2). Railway companies and shipping lines commissioned many such posters, mainly for advertising purposes – for example Cassandre's work in 1927 for the *Étoile du Nord* train service (Paris to Amsterdam via Brussels).

As for the car, it is not surprising that it provided one of the favourite subjects for magazines. Synonymous with liberty, leisure, luxury and travel, its particularly American tinge gave a touch of both elegance (5) and extravagance (6) to magazine covers. There is also its dual relationship with women. Although its sleek, feminine lines have often been associated with a macho aesthetic where skimpily clad or topless pin-up girls pose with various vehicles for calendars and posters, from the end of the 1950s the car has also become associated with women's growing independence (4, 8), providing car manufacturers with a distinct market for their products.

1. *Life*. Cover, Paul Gogld, 14th January 1909. 2. *L'Air*. January 1937. 3. *Lectures Pour Tous*. Cover, G. Dutriac, January 1931. 4. *AAT*. October 1958. 5. *L'Illustration*. Cover, Guy Sabran, 3rd October 1931. 6. *Paris Match*. Cover, François Pagès, 6th October 1962. 7. *Life*. Cover, Broughton, 28th December 1911. 8. *Kristall*. Photography, Walter Hennig. Cover, M.von Glinski, 2nd quarter 1959.

The Rise of Sport

Magnifying the human body, arousing our feelings, crowning heroes and characterised by success as much as beauty, sport excites the masses and the press. Unpredictable by nature, sport offers a profusion of images, only one of which might capture the essence of the moment. For an athlete's profession is a highly precise one, with success hinging on the perfect movement, a millimetre more or less or a second gained or lost. A photographer must be able to capture that instant just as precisely as the athlete. Destinies hang in the balance, and readers avidly devour these moments of grace.

'The dash of a winger down the touchline is like that of a gazelle! And what about the force of the front-line in the midst of the scrum, the power of the muscles, the thighs; it's magnificent!' exclaimed Jean Lacouture, a veteran reporter for *Le Monde* and *Le Nouvel Observateur,* talking about rugby. Capturing the beauty of such moments is a true challenge for the sports photographer.

It is not by chance that the histories of sport and photography are so intrinsically linked. Sports photography has always provided ample opportunities for all kinds of experimentation. And both sport and the press excel at creating powerful events. But although today sport has become the popular activity *par excellence,* up until the 20th century it interested only the army and snobs!

English Origins

The first French sports magazine was launched by Eugène Chapus in 1850. It was called *Le Sport, Journal des Gens du Monde* (Sport, the Magazine for Cosmopolitans). In 1866 Léon Crémière, who had an eye for the latest vogue, launched *Le Centaure,* an illustrated magazine covering sport, hunting, farming and the arts.

The word 'sport' is a relatively recent one, originating in England, where inter-school and university sporting competitions have long been organised, while in France only the anglophile aristocracy entertained themselves by kicking a ball around or parading

dressed up to the nines on horseback. Disderi, Nadar, Delton and Pierre Petit all set up their equestrian photography studios in the Bois de Boulogne, just outside Paris. People would come to have their photographs taken, sitting on a hired horse.

Tennis as we know it today was codified by Major Walter Wingfield in 1874, while rugby became popular with the first international matches in 1906. Although a set of rules for football was firmly drawn up in 1863, it only became the popular international sport it is today after the Second World War. As for gymnastics and skiing, they were initially the preserve of the military.

Waiting for Kodak

Meanwhile, photography was developing. In France, Étienne Jules Marey had already been making his deconstructive studies of movement since 1869. His work was continued by the American Edward Muybridge, who placed a number of cameras along a race course, each one's shutter mechanism linked to a string that a galloping horse would break, successively triggering a series of photographs. The experiment was conclusive, capturing the animal in mid gallop with its four hooves tucked up under its body, breaking all pictorial traditions.

In 1881 the City of Paris lent Marey the Parc des Princes stadium for him to stage his experiments. The end of the 19th century saw the popularisation of both photography and sport with the arrival of the first Kodak camera

1. *L'Autre Journal.* Cover (Magic Johnson)., Annie Leibovitz/Contact Press Images, 25th June 1992. Art Director, Agnès Cruz. **2.** *Life.* Cover, A.P., 25th April 1938. Art Director, Howard Richmond. **3.** *Punch.* 29th May 1957. **4.** *The New Yorker.* Cover "Poised", by Kenton Nelson, 19th to 26th June 2000. **5.** *Life.* Cover "Méthode Française de Ski Technique", Emile Allais. Edition Flèche. Photo, Pierre Boucher, 24th January 1949. Art Director, Charles Tudor.

Overleaf
6. *New York Times Magazine.* 18th October 1964. **7.** *Sport Illustrated.* Cover, Greg Foster, 31st January 2000. Art Director, Edward P.Truscio

The New York Times
Magazine

October 18, 1964   SECTION E

TOKYO ● 1964

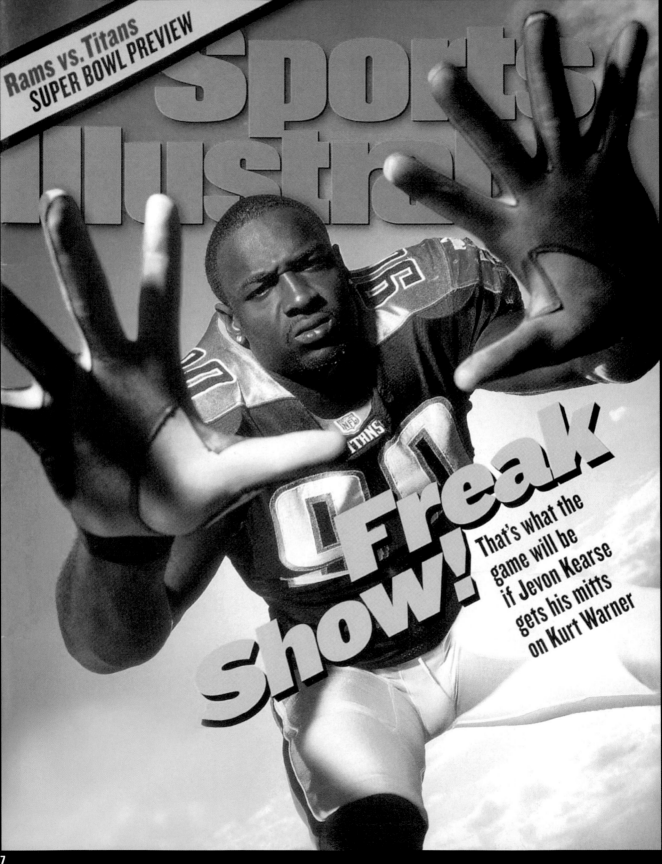

Rams vs. Titans
SUPER BOWL PREVIEW

Sports
Illustr

Freak
Show!

That's what the
game will be
if Jevon Kearse
gets his mitts
on Kurt Warner

in 1888 and in 1896 for the first time since 369 AD, the Olympic games were celebrated in Athens.

Birth of the Reporter

The first sports reporter is relatively unknown. He was a Frenchman called Jules Beau. A specialist in 'sports, equestrian and cycling photography', he started making his expertise pay in 1894, compiling a veritable pantheon of the sporting stars of the time. Whether in track or road competitions he followed these heroes everywhere. His work was published in *La Vie au grand air* (Life in the Great Outdoors) and *La Bicyclette*. Since the invention of pedals by Pierre Michaud in 1861, the bicycle had become a real hit, first of all for the bourgeoisie, then, as cheaper models became available, for the wider public. A growing specialised press was not far behind. But this press was not content to simply recount sporting events. Publications soon realised the great advantages of creating their own. After all, the press depended on sport for its survival and profit and vice versa. The great competitions like the cycling Tour de France, the Le Mans 24 hour automobile race, the football European Cup and skiing World Cup were all dreamt up by sporting publications, starting with the Paris-Rouen cycling race, which was organised by *Le Vélocipède Illustré* in 1869, vélocipède being the original French term for these two-wheeled contraptions.

The 1920s and 1930s saw a massive growth in sporting literature. The improvements in photographic film and technology enabled photojournalists to follow matches and races much more closely. Among these new press heroes were the Austrian Lothar Rübelt, himself an athlete and one of the first users of the new lighter equipment like Ermanox and Leica cameras; the Frenchman Jacques Henri Lartigue; the Hungarians Kertész and Martin Munkacsi, who worked for *A.Z. Sport;* the Swiss Lothar Jeck of *Schweitzer Illustri-erte,* who was one of the first to undertake complete reportages of competitions; and a host of others including Salomon, Weber, Eisenstaedt, F. H. Man, Bosshard, Paul Senn, Hans Staub, André Steiner, Emeric Feher and François Kollar. Then there were the artists of the constructivist movement, who used the

LIFE

400 METER SWIMMING CHAMPION

REG. U. S. PAT. OFF.

20 CENTS

AUGUST 20, 1951

CIRCULATION OVER 5,200,000

1

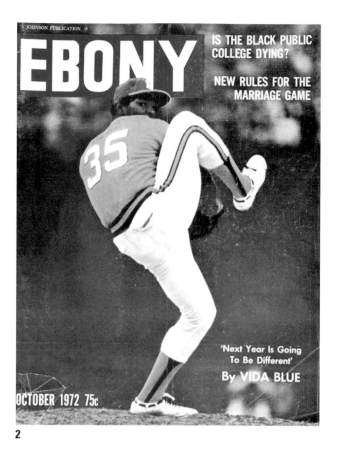

2

3

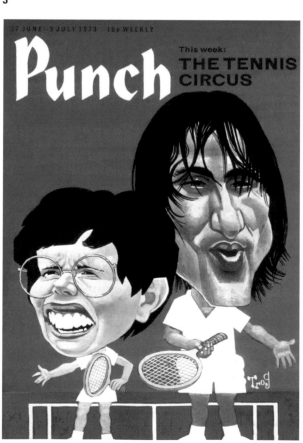

4

5

image of the athlete for their creative research, from Moholy-Nagy to Rodchenko, Baumeistera and Paladini. Throughout a Europe scarred by the Great War sport became a source of pleasure and reconciliation with life.

Muscle Culture

In the 1930s photojournalism made spectacular progress thanks to technological innovations like the small format, flash lamps and roll-film. The press continued to prosper and agencies sprouted. Sport was becoming a true cult, encouraging all media to devote more space to it. *Vu, Regards, L'Illustration, Weekly Illustrated, Picture Post* and *Life* filled their pages with all kinds of sports reporting; everything was there, from the exciting to the dramatic to the strange. Sporting imagery also spilled over into other areas, particularly fashion, and was a noticeable influence on the image given by Martin Munkacsi to *Harper's Bazaar* from 1934. After the Second World War magazines like *Life* and *Paris-Match* turned sporting champions into celebrities as huge as cinema stars. Ernst Haas, Eisenstaedt, Dominis, Ralph Morse, Steinheimer, Gjon Mili and Georg Silk ardently pursued perfection, producing powerful images that had considerable impact. In 1960 the Olympic Games, which took place in Rome, were broadcast worldwide for the very first time. The sportsman was elevated to the heights of a demigod, adored and imitated both as an achiever of startling exploits and as a performer. Sport and the media drew ever closer, with television dictating the timetable of events at the Olympic Games. One might very well wonder if sport, a vehicle of drama, of values and a philosophy of life had not become just another hoarding for advertisers to display their slogans.

1. *Life.* Cover, Leonard McCombe, 20th September 1951. Art Director, Charles Tudor. 2. *Ebony.* (Charles O. Finger). Cover, Don Sparks, October 1972. Art Director, Herbert Temple. 3. *Life.* Cover, A.Y. Owen, 29th April 1957. Art Director, Charles Tudor. 4. *The Saturday Evening Post.* Cover, Constantin Alajalov, 23rd October 1948. Art Director, Kenneth Stuart. 5. *Punch.* 3rd July 1973.

A Married Man's Fantasy

She could very well have remained a plain little bourgeois girl from the chic Passy quarter of Paris. Her parents, firmly attached to the quiet cosiness of their unremarkable life, imagined her as a ballerina, discreet and reserved. But at 14, she who would one day invade the subconscious of millions made her first appearance as cover girl, for *Jardin des Modes.* Although her family was less than enthusiastic about it, they agreed, but on one condition, that only the initials BB would appear under the photos.

BB Supernova

The BB phenomenon quickly spun out of her parents' control. In May 1949 Brigitte's face graced the cover of *Elle,* where the potential of this young beauty was recognised immediately. She embarked upon a brief career as a model, before making her cinema debut in 1952 under the direction of Jean Boyer, who had been fascinated by her devil-or-angel ambiguity while leafing through a women's magazine. The film was *Le Trou Normand,* starring Bourvil. The following year Willy Rozier, Sacha Guitry, René Clair and Marc Allégret all rushed to work with her. A darling of the press, men dreamed about her and

1

2

3

4

5

6

7

8

9

10

11

women dreamed of being her. Thanks to his network of journalist friends Roger Vadim, her first husband, was able to guarantee unprecedented media support for her, particularly at *Paris Match*. He never stopped telling her: 'You will become the unattainable fantasy of married men'. It was he who sent her soaring to the heights of fame in *And God Created Woman*. She personified carefree youthful sensuality, garnering apoplectically outraged adulation from the British press , which called her 'sex kitten' or 'little gazelle'.

Bardot Worship

Brigitte vaunted her sexuality, causing quite a stir at the time, but she never neglected her very proper upbringing. Her impertinence and the frankness of some of her declarations upset the moral applecart and made her a darling of the media. Jean Cocteau, Simone de Beauvoir and Marguerite Duras all wrote articles about her. But the rather more traditional French press fretted about her influence on 'our young girls', who needless to say all copied her style. She was spoken of in legendary terms, even giving rise to a new word, *bardolâtrie*, or Bardot worship. Jean-Luc Godard cast her in *Le Mépris* (Contempt), Serge Gainsbourg wrote songs for her, while for Charles de Gaulle and the people of France she was Marianne, the incarnation of republican beauty.

Then, in 1973, after three marriages, fifty films and fifteen hit singles, she bowed out of show business saying: 'I am leaving cinema so that cinema does not leave me', overseeing from afar the dismantling of her legend while surrounded by her menagerie of pet animals.

1. *Paris Match.* Photo, J. Dussart/Rapho, 21st September 1984. Art Director, Guy Trillat. 2. *Elle.* Photo, William Connors, 22nd April 1960. Head of art and graphics department, Peter Knapp. Art Director, Roger Giret. 3. *Cinémonde.* Photo, Sam Levin, 15th May 1958. 4. *Ciné Revue.* 13th May 1976. 5. *Mon Film.* 25th June 1958. 6. *Cinémonde.* Photo, J. Dussart/Rapho, 5th April 1966. 7. *Elle.* Photo, J.P. Bonnotte/Gamma, 29th June 1967. 8. *Cinémonde.* 20th October 1955. 9. *Lui.* Cover, Aslan, March 1973. 10. *Vogue Hommes.* Photo, Willy Rizzo, July–August 1992. Art Director, Jean-Jacques Driewir. 11. *Paris Match.* 2nd June 1961.

Overleaf
12. *Paris Match.* Photo, J. Dussart, 29th December 1962.
13. *Jours de France.* 14th to 20th January 1984.

PARIS MATCH

N° 716 / 29 DÉC. 1962 / 1 NF

EXCLUSIF

OUI C'EST BB

**POUR LE
NOUVEL AN BRIGITTE
SE DÉGUISE EN
DIVA**

Aigrette, pendants d'oreilles,
robe de dentelle, mouchoir de batiste,
face-à-main et partition de musique : c'est la
parfaite panoplie de la cantatrice
de sous-préfecture. C'est celle aussi qu'a
choisie Brigitte Bardot pour l'un des
nombreux gags de son « show »
télévisé du nouvel an (9 chansons et
1 ballet). Lequel devient une
tradition. Voir notre avant-première
à l'intérieur.

J. DUSSART

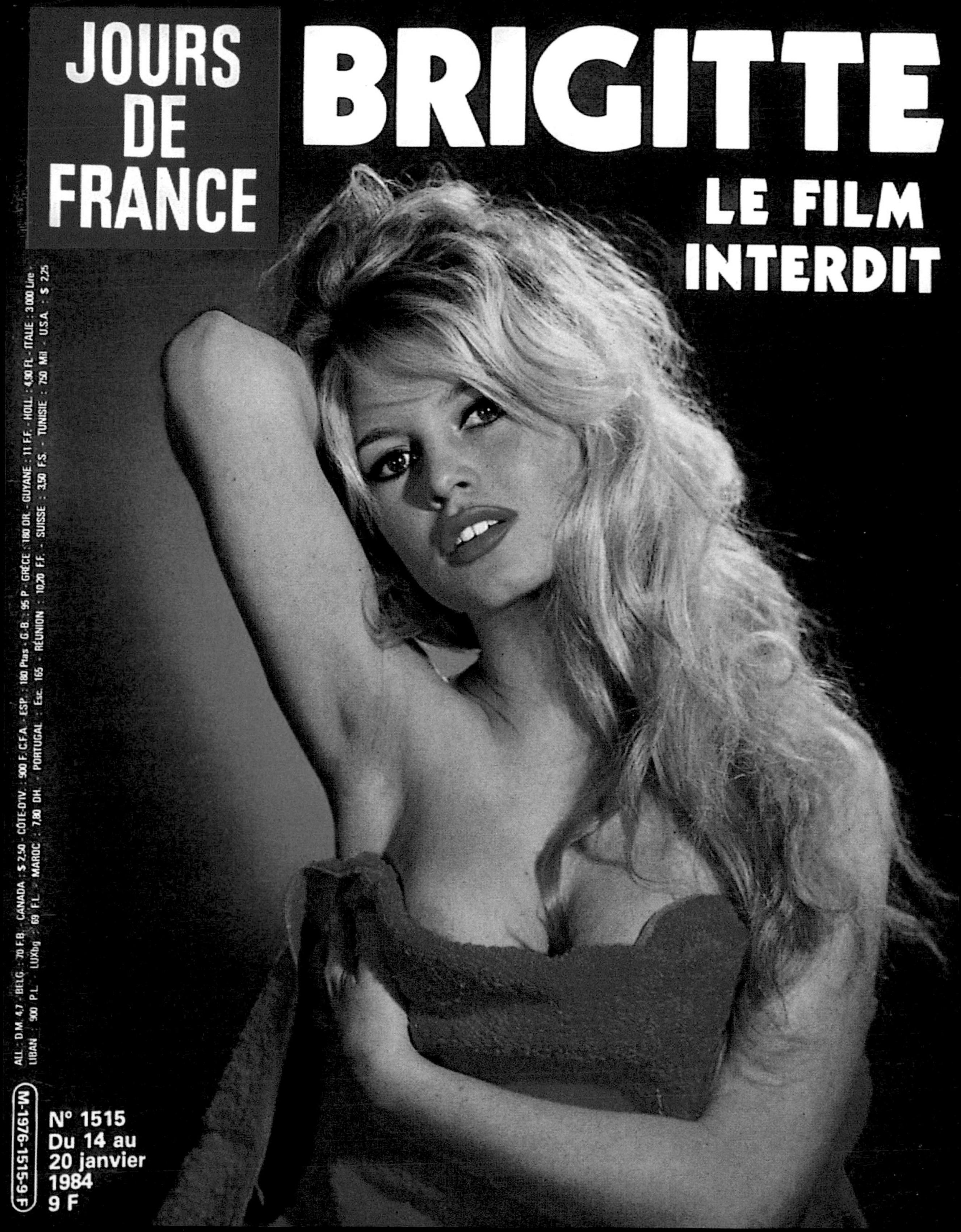

JOURS
DE
FRANCE

BRIGITTE
LE FILM INTERDIT

ALL : D.M. 4,7 · BELG : 70 F.B. · CANADA : $ 2,50 · CÔTE-D'IV : 900 F.C.F.A. · ESP : 180 Ptas · G.-B. : 95 P · GRÈCE : 180 DR. · GUYANE : 11 F.F. · HOLL : 4,90 FL · ITALIE : 3 000 Lire · LIBAN : 900 P.L. · LUXbg : 69 F.L. · MAROC : 7,80 DH · PORTUGAL : Esc. 165 · RÉUNION : 10,20 F.F. · SUISSE : 3,50 FS · TUNISIE : 750 Mil · USA : $ 2,25

[M-1976-1515-9 F]

N° 1515
Du 14 au
20 janvier
1984
9 F

13

The Last Stars of the Black & White Era

Pioneers of modern pop music, surfing the libertarian wave of the 60s with finesse and talent, The Beatles were deftly in tune with their time and in just a decade they became the most popular group in the history of pop music. Paul McCartney, John Lennon, George Harrison and Ringo Starr saw their career soar in October 1962 when their first single, *Love Me Do/PS I Love You* was released, reaching number 17 in the charts. Insolent yet charming, the four lads from Liverpool attracted the kids while not offending the sensibilities of their parents.

Beatlemania

In February 1963 their first album *Please, Please Me* sat at the top of the charts for 8 months, before being replaced by *With the Beatles,* their second album. The whole of Britain was caught up in the craze, from blue collar to royalty. The demonstration of hysterical adulation by thousands of fans in front of the London Palladium on the 13th of October 1963 was widely covered in the papers the next day, and the term *beatlemania* was coined. *The Times,* the traditional voice of the establishment, was the first serious paper to publish a glowing article, while on the 29th of December 1963 *The Sunday Times* called John Lennon and Paul McCartney 'the greatest composers since Beethoven'. They even received MBEs from Her Majesty. But despite this sign of royal approval, The Beatles's success was still perceived as a social phenomenon by the general public, their image largely restricted to that of four mop-tops mobbed by hysterical fans at Heathrow, and not as worthy musicians in their own right.

After conquering Europe it was the turn of the United States to welcome The Beatles, with *I Want To Hold Your Hand,* released in 1964, totalling 30 million sales in just fifteen weeks as the Fab Four appeared on the covers of *Newsweek, Life, Look, Time* and even *Playboy.* Momentarily shifting its focus from fashion *Vogue* printed a full page photo of them. All their concerts sold out as fast as tickets were put on sale. Every appearance made tabloid

1

PUNCH 23 NOVEMBER 1966
ONE SHILLING & SIXPENCE

A BEATLE talks to Patrick Catling

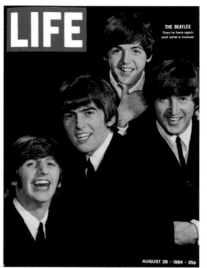

3

4

1. *Salut les Copains.* Cover, Richard Avedon, March 1968. **2.** *Punch.* 23rd November 1966. **3.** *Life.* Cover, John Dominis, 28th August 1964. Art Director, Bernard Quint. **4.** *Rolling Stone.* 15th July 1976. **5.** *The Sunday Times Magazine.* 29th March 1981.

5

headlines. 'The Beatles are more popular than Jesus Christ,' declared John Lennon in 1966, provoking outrage across the devoutly religious South of the United States.

Counter-Cultural Icons

After a final concert at Candlestick Park in San Francisco on the 29th of August 1966, The Beatles stopped touring and disappeared into the studio to explore new musical avenues. The result was *Sergent Pepper's Lonely Hearts Club Band,* considered one of the best pop records ever made and earning them the respect of their peers. Not only was their music more ambitious, so was their ideology. In just a few years they had became front line figures in the burgeoning counter-culture of the late 1960s, preaching a philosophy of love, peace, spiritual discovery and social change, denouncing the Vietnam War and confessing their use of recreational drugs. Despite drawing the fire of conservative critics and the establishment press who had once praised them, their place was assured as the cultural reference of an entire generation.

From Myth to Martyr

Dissension within the group was revealed soon after the death of their manager Brian Epstein. Though recorded before *Abbey Road, Let it Be* (1970) is considered to be the group's farewell album. Beyond general stupefaction and a host of far-fetched theories, the break-up of The Beatles at the height of their glory was interpreted by the media as a sign that the optimism of the Swinging Sixties was perhaps drawing to a close, although the group's mythic status was assured. On the 8th of December 1980 John Lennon was shot dead and the myth took on the added dimension of martyrdom. Not long before, the charismatic singer-songwriter had declared that the meaning of life was to 'be here now'. We would do well to remember it.

FOUR LADS LIKELY TO SUCCEED

1

2

ALVIN LEE

POSTERS : BRYAN FERRY

3

4

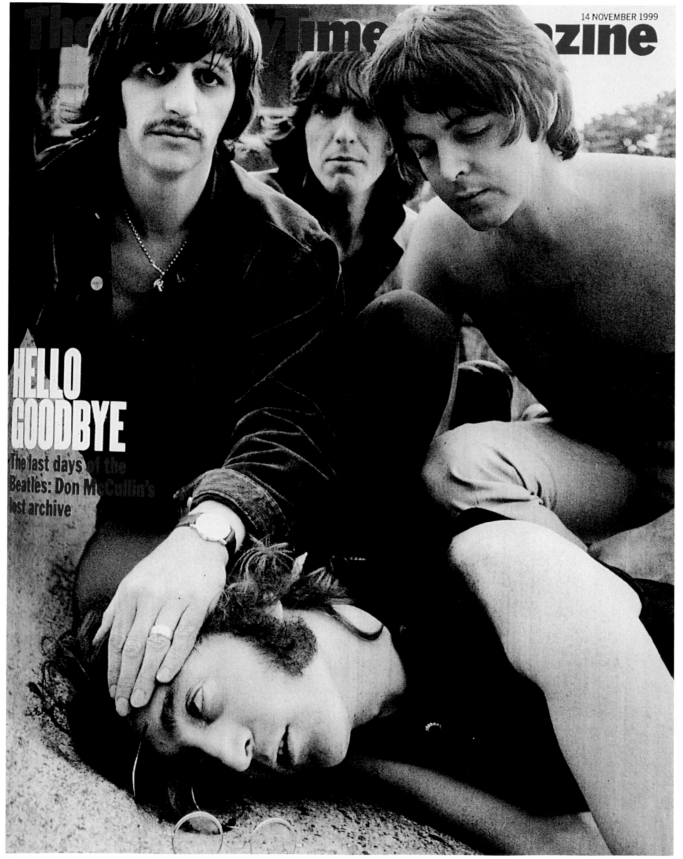

14 NOVEMBER 1999

**HELLO
GOODBYE**

The last days of the
Beatles: Don McCullin's
lost archive

5

1. *Stern.* 1964. **2.** *The Sunday
Times Magazine.* 1st September
1968. **3.** *Best.* Janvier 1975. **4.**
The Sunday Times Magazine.
2nd September 2001. **5.** *The
Sunday Times Magazine.*
14th November 1999.

The Final Triumph of the Old Lion

Most magazine covers of Winston Churchill picture him as an international statesman. Yet at the age of 66, when he became Prime Minister of a Britain at war, Churchill had had more downs than ups in his political career. His rise had been brilliant though, including an appointment to the highly strategic post of First Lord of the Admiralty at the start of the First World War when he was not yet forty.

Things turned sour with the failure of the Dardanelles expedition, which he had largely promoted. Discredited, he resigned from his post and was somewhat at a loss when the war ended, adrift in a world that had changed and left him behind. A largely unrepentant Conservative, despite crossing the floor to the Liberals for a while, he fought against reformist projects and, as Chancellor of the Exchequer from 1924-1929 in Baldwin's Conservative government, was responsible for Britain's disastrous return to the pre-war gold standard. Long marginalised on the right of the Conservative Party because of his anti-Communist and anti-Nazi stance, everything changed as the war loomed. The prescience of his reactionary bellicosity was, alas, recognised too late. Chamberlain's appeasement may have bought Britain a little time, but when the guns started to roar he was soon out of his depth. In May 1940, Churchill became Prime Minister.

Cigars and V for Victory

Churchill quickly galvanised the whole country with his determination, his energy and a number of heroic declarations. From then on, the press's attitude towards him underwent a complete about-face, now portraying Churchill as the symbol of Britain's resistance against Hitler. Fortunately for them, Churchill was a photographer's dream, with his ever-present bow tie (6), black hat (3,5) and cigar (1,3,4). Best known of all perhaps is his V for Victory, formed by the index and middle fingers and widely imitated ever since. Whatever the vicissitudes of his political life, in the eyes of the world Churchill remains perhaps the most respected British statesman ever.

PICTURE POST

THE MAN IN CHARGE

HULTON'S NATIONAL WEEKLY

President Benes talks to Picture Post:

VICTORY... AND THEN? 4D

MAY 27, 1944   Vol. 23. No. 9

1

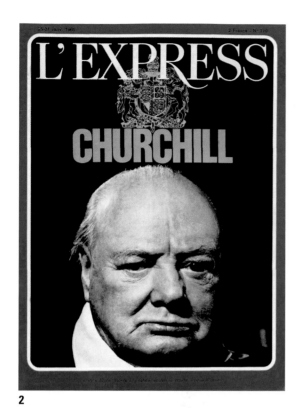

2

3

4

5

6

7

1. *Picture Post*. 27th May 1944. **2. *L'Express*.** Photo, Magnum, 25th to 31st January 1965. Art director, André Gobert. **3. *Jours de France*.** 25th November to 1st December 1954. **4. *Life*.** Photo, Hans Wild, 7th January 1946. **5. *Picture Post*.** 25th May 1940. **6. *Life*.** Photo, Karsh, 21st May 1945. **7. *Paris Match*.** Photo, Karsh, 31st January 1965.

Prime Target of the *Paparazzi*

The story of Diana Spencer is that of a fairytale gone wrong. Killed in a car crash in Paris on the 31st of August 1997 at the age of 36, she had been the prime obsession of the world's press for 17 years, a true heroine straight out of the tradition of *Paris Match*.

Born on the 31st of July 1961 into one of the grandest families of the British aristocracy, Diana apparently wanted for nothing: she had a fortune, a noble title and youthful beauty. Although a mediocre pupil at some of the finest English and Swiss schools, she set her heart on what she hoped would provide true happiness: marrying her Prince Charming. And she succeeded. Upon the announcement of her engagement to the heir to the throne at the tender age of 19, all of Britain fell under the charm of this young blushing slightly shy girl. 'The greatest marriage ever!' screamed the headlines. Charles and Diana made history on their wedding day, the 29th of July 1981, when they exchanged a long kiss on the balcony at Buckingham Palace, so melting the heart of the whole planet. The unauthorised photo made all the front pages, heralding a new era for the House of Windsor. It was the furthest that a member of the royal family had gone in shamelessly displaying the romantic affection and sensitivity of one of Her Majesty's ordinary subjects.

Gilded Cage

Every public appearance brought renewed pleasure and wonderment to her as she was rapturously received wherever she went. Through her the royal family attained a much needed appearance of humanity, warmth and spontaneity. 'The loveliest child' exclaimed the press when her first child William was born, followed in 1984 by Harry. But the honeymoon was short-lived. Prince and Princess simply did not have enough in common. Diana slipped into depression and the marriage was soon on the rocks. The press lunged into competitive

1. *Paris Match.* Photo Cardinal/Sygma, 25th September 1997. Art director, Guy Trillat. 2. *Maclean's.* Photo Hussein/Sipa, 15th June 1992. Art director, Nick Burnett. 3. *Paris Match.* 24th July 1997. 4. *Sunday Telegraph Magazine.* 18th April 1982.

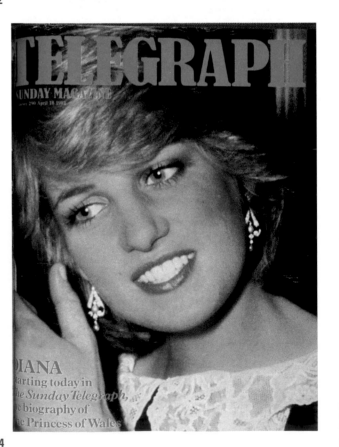

5

6

Diana
FOR EVER

10

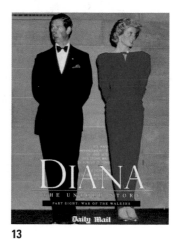

12   13

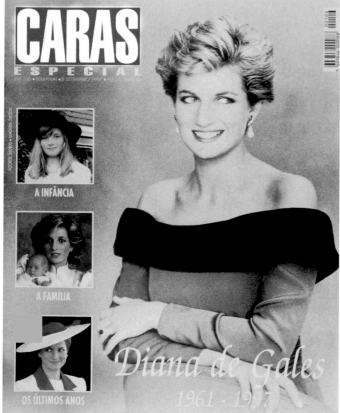

7

11

8   9

hyperbole: 'the saddest of break-ups'; 'the blackest treachery'; 'the cruellest loneliness'. Their respective infidelities were exposed and dissected, spiced up with revealing photos. Separation was officially announced in Parliament on the 10th of December 1992, with official divorce pronounced on the 28th of August 1996.

Princess of a Thousand Faces

She liked to ring the changes with hair, outfits, hats, countries, and sometimes men. Princess, wife, mother, daughter-in-law, lover and ambassador for worthy causes, each magazine picked up on the facet that suited it. Appearing in a swimsuit with the same poise and grace she would radiate when wearing an evening gown, snapped at a private moment or posing in public, alone or with her family, in the midst of a crowd or holding the hand of Mother Teresa, whose battle for the poor of Calcutta she supported, nothing could hold the shutterbugs back. More! More! the readers seemed to cry. When she fell in love with Dodi, the paparazzi could hardly keep up. Her tragic death in a Paris underpass only immortalised the myth that still surrounds her.

5. *Daily Mail.* 6. *Gente Nova.* 3rd to 9th September 1997. 7. *Caras Especial.* Photo, Sygma, 8th September 1997. 8. *Bunte.* 9th June 1993. 9. *Mulher Moderna.* 11th to 17th September 1997. 10. *Le Figaro Magazine.* Photo , Mario Testino, 22nd August 1998. Art Director, Joël Pradines. 11. *You.* Photo, Mario Testino, 23rd August 1998. Art Director, Linda Boyle. 12. *Punch.* 6th July 1990. 13. *Daily Mail.*

Overleaf
14. *Sunday Telegraph Magazine.* 12th May 1985. 15. *Time.* Photo Mario Testino, 15th September 1997.

TELEGRAPH

SUNDAY MAGAZINE

mber 446 May 12 1985

SPECIAL REPORT
ROYAL TOUR
OF ITALY

14

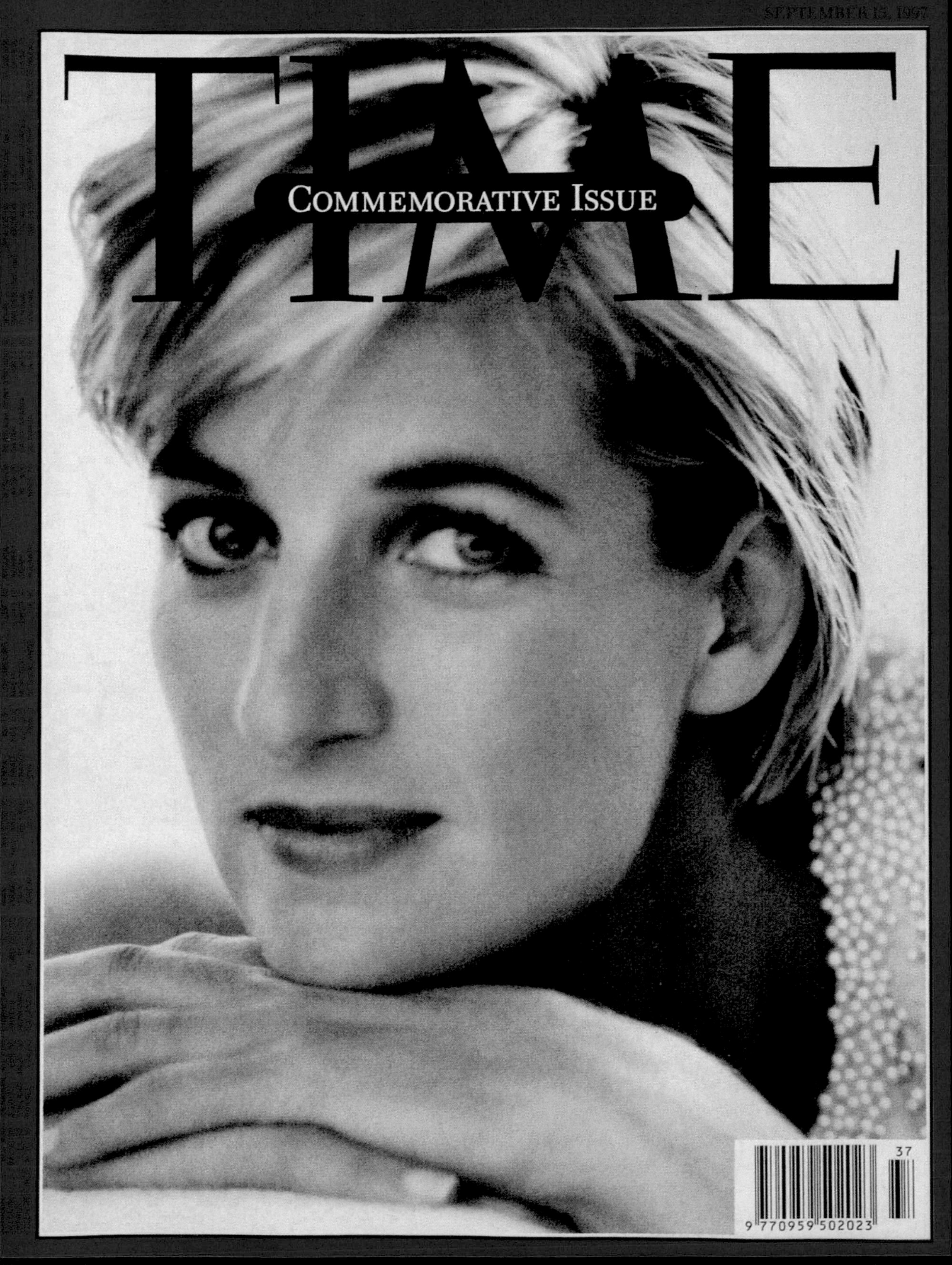

TIME

COMMEMORATIVE ISSUE

37

9 770959 502023

From Angel to Myth

The unforgettable Berliner was born in 1901 not long after the beginning of cinema itself and died just before the 1992 Cannes Film Festival that paid tribute to her. To the last journalist she agreed to see before the seclusion she chose during the last ten years of her life, she summed up her career thus: 'At twenty I was nothing. At eighty I'm just an ordinary old woman. In between I was an actress. There's nothing else to say.' Except that this particular actress had an erotic charge that stirred the imagination of an entire era.

When Josef von Sternberg discovered her and cast her in *The Blue Angel* in 1930, she had already acted in twenty-odd German comedies and had even considered abandoning the cinema to fulfil her first ambition buying a farm. and raising a family. But the character of Lola Lola changed her life forever, and she became the *femme fatale,* corseted in black, singing throatily 'Ich bin von Kopf zu Fuß auf Liebe eingestellt' ('From head to toe I am made for love'). Her languorous sensuality annoyed some, enflamed most and guaranteed the film's success.

Garbo's Rival

While Marlene Dietrich characterised perverse, unfathomable seduction, Greta Garbo, her rival, symbolised beauty that was enigmatic but human. Dietrich cultivated artifice and ambiguity, launching the vogue of androgynous creatures, dream women wearing smoking jackets and top hats. She penetrated and fascinated Hollywood under the aegis of her protector and Pygmalion, Sternberg, with whom she made five other films, pieces of refined eroticism. North Africa (*Morocco*) and China (*Shanghai Express*), reconstructed in the studio, served as backdrops for her sophisticated allure. Dietrich would find it hard to leave behind her glamorous persona, even when she stopped working with Sternberg after the relative failure of *The Devil Is A Woman* which they made in 1935, in which she donned an astounding panoply of feathers, wigs and sequins.

Her distant beauty was no longer paying off. On the advice of Paramount, she changed

1

2

3

4

5

6

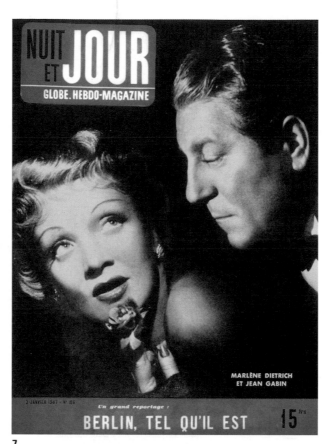

7

8

styles, accepting more prosaic roles, including westerns, which revealed other facets of her acting talent. She made another thirty films and gained even more popularity during the Second World War. Although attached to her country of origin, she was hostile to Hitler's Nazi regime and refused all of Goebbels's invitations to return to Germany, even participating in an anti-Nazi campaign. She made a long tour to support allied soldiers in the front line, singing one of her greatest hits, *Lili Marlene,* in English.

Nostalgia for the *Femme Fatale*

In 1946 she was madly in love with the French leading man Jean Gabin and agreed to star with him in *Martin Roumagnac,* directed by Georges Lacombe. Her role was considered to be against type but echoed the dreams of her youth, that of a petit bourgeois wife in a steamy kitchen, for that was how Gabin loved her. In the 1950s she graced the screen much less frequently, preferring singing tours where she attempted to recreate the legendary Marlene of the 1930s, in a sheath dress slit to the waist. But it is in her cameo role as the world-weary yet steely madam in Orson Welles's 1958 film *Touch of Evil* that she truly steals the picture. She appeared in two final feature films in 1961 and 1978, before retiring from public life to end her days in Paris. But her sensual voice and seductive gaze will haunt viewers for as long as the silver screen continues to shine.

1. *Stern*. 1992. 2. *Der Stern*. 1948. 3. *Der Stern*. 1954. 4. *Cinévie*. 9th April 1946. 5. *Der Stern*. 1950. 6. *Cinémonde*. Photo, Paramount, 24th August 1933. 7. *Nuit et Jour*. 2nd January 1947. 8. *V*. 27 October 1946.

General and President

In June 1940 Charles de Gaulle was just a lowly junior minister in the last government of France's Third Republic. During the five years of his exile in London, occupied France knew the Head of the Free French only through his voice broadcast over the radio.

De Gaulle soon learned how to use the media. Force of circumstance made him intimately acquainted with the radio, then the printed press and finally television. Inspired by the English, he transformed the press conference into a kind of grand show that explained his policies clearly, intended more for the television viewers themselves than the assembled journalists actually present.

The Two Faces of Charles de Gaulle

De Gaulle presents two different images that correspond to his two periods of political activity: the de Gaulle of 1945 and the de Gaulle of 1958-1969. In his first period of political activity he was a member of the Resistance and then Head of Provisional Government; he completely reorganised the country upon Liberation, before withdrawing from politics to leave the various political parties to the intrigues and games that he so disapproved of. The first de Gaulle is depicted in uniform and kepi, since his legitimacy lay in his struggle against Nazi Germany and France's collaboration. In the prime of life, tall, svelte and dark, he very nearly fitted the image of a prospective dictator that his enemies sought to portray

Ambiance

DIRECTEUR GÉNÉRAL : JACQUES GAISSER ● 2ᵉ ANNÉE - NUMÉRO 8 - 31 JANVIER 1945 ● DIRECTEUR POLITIQUE : PIERRE-BLOCH

10ᶠ

Cet enfant a sauvé la France !

(Voir page 3)

TIME
THE WEEKLY NEWSMAGAZINE

DE GAULLE
Already the ruler incredible of the French Empire—by courage.

JOURS DE FRANCE

Ses compagnons, dépositaires de sa pensée, sauront la transmettre à la jeunesse de France.

1   2   3

5

6

him as. Then came the wilderness years when de Gaulle disappeared from the media. 'I am not going to start my career as a dictator at the age of 67', he declared. Thirteen years later, in 1958, the statesman revealed himself in the guise of the old sage one turns to in times of trouble. With what hair he had left, and his moustache now snow-white, his bearing was still just as imposing, but his now portly figure had taken on a stoop. De Gaulle had abandonned his characteristic uniform and kepi and would only dust them off at key moments of national crisis, such as the putsch of the generals in Algeria. The President's rivals had hoped that once elected he would content himself with performing ceremonial duties, but they greatly underestimated him. In fact de Gaulle galvanised the country, presiding over its economic recovery and revolutionising foreign policy.

The last photos show him walking on an Irish beach with a cane, but the most striking image is undoubtedly the drawing by Jacques Faizant that pictures de Gaulle as a felled oak beneath which Marianne (the personification of the Republic) sits weeping.

1. *Time.* Cover, Ernest Hamlin Baker, 4th August 1941.
2. *Jours de France.* 23rd November 1970. 3. *Ambiance.* 31st January 1945. 4. *Life.* Photo, Karsh, 13th November 1944. 5. *Paris Match.* 1st June 1962. 6. *Paris Match.* Photo, Paul Slade, 21st November 1970.

A Monster in the Media

Contrary to Communism, Nazism is not political ideology but dogma, whose sole tenet is racism. All other parts of it are inspired by and changed according to circumstance. That is its strength. Passionately convinced of the superiority of the Aryan race, Adolf Hitler fully committed himself to demonstrating this through a policy of power, war and extermination. Purification through violence; the revolution of nihilism.

Apart from his political instinct and intuition, Hitler's skills as an orator were unquestionable. They were magnified during huge militaristic rallies whose high point was the Führer's speech, also broadcast over the radio. When he became Chancellor he created a Ministry of Propaganda. In 1929 he wrote in the paper *Der Angriff:* 'When propaganda has filled an entire people with a single idea, administration can be left to a handful of men.'

In the German Press

Joseph Goebbels, Minister of Information and Propaganda gave daily instructions to the newspapers and organised regular press conferences to ensure harmony and provide the themes that he wished to be covered. He wanted ideas that were simple but strong, that played upon emotions, obfuscated thought and were understood by the largest number of people.

'Hitler is Germany.' This slogan conveyed several meanings. The Führer was portrayed as the head of a family, indeed he was often shown surrounded by women and children. He was also the providential head of Germany, with his chest stuck out, his steady gaze and firm expression (4, 6). 'One Country, One People, One Führer' was another slogan.

In the Foreign Press

The attitude of the foreign press was unequivocal. While Mussolini and his Fascism were initially attractive, Hitler and his methods were immediately condemned and his double-talk was soon revealed for what it was. The news-rich British press was soon banned in Germany. In the French press Hitler was universally condemned, but opinion on how to

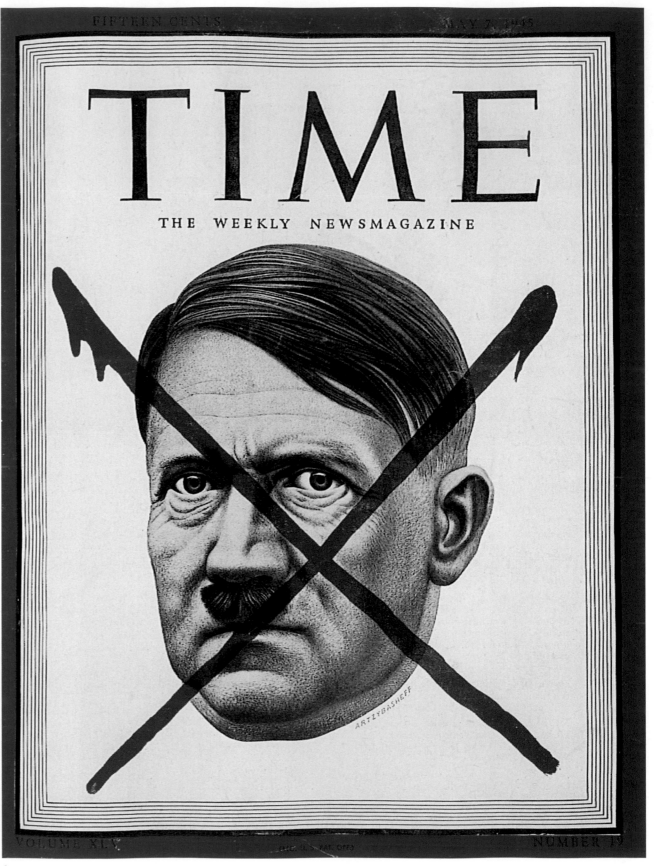

1

2

3

4

5

6

deal with him was more divided. Up until 1935 the Left was pacifist and refused to acknowledge the growing threat, while the nationalist Right was anti-German by nature. After the Moscow-induced change of direction in the French Communist Party and the rise of the Popular Front, the struggle against Fascism became a priority for the Left. As for the nationalist Right, it switched from its previous anti-German stance and influenced by the authoritarian and anti-Communist character of the Nazi regime, became pacifist in turn.

1. *Time.* Cover by Artzybasheff, 7th May 1945. **2.** *Die Woche.* 1st January 1941. **3.** *Picture Post.* 16th December 1939. **4.** *Vu.* Photo Keystone, 8th February 1933. **5.** *L'Express.* 22nd to 28th August 1977. Art directors, Tharcise Ruyer and Guillaume Marcilhacy. **6.** *Der Spiegel.* 29th January 1964.

Shooting star

Born in Philadelphia in 1929, Grace Kelly started appearing as a model on magazine covers such as *Cosmopolitan* and *Redbook* to pay for acting classes. After two successful films she signed a seven-year contract in 1953 with Metro Goldwyn Mayer, working alongside the biggest stars like Clark Gable and Ava Gardner. But it was Alfred Hitchcock who really made her a star, firstly in *Dial M For Murder*, then in *Rear Window*.

In May 1955 she was invited to the Cannes Film Festival for the showing of Georgie Elgin's film *The Country Girl*. The magazine *Paris Match* organised a meeting with Prince Rainier of Monaco. It was love at first sight. Without knowing it the magazine had not only concocted a photo reportage for their next issue, they had also given birth to a saga that would continue to feed the press and *Paris Match* in particular, for several decades to come.

'The marriage of the century!' proclaimed the headlines in April 1956. The wedding took place with great pomp in the cathedral of Saint-Nicholas, lasting for three hours, with six hundred guests, three million television viewers, and the ever-present Metro Goldwyn Mayer using and abusing its rights to shoot

1

2

JOURS DE FRANCE

SEMAINE DU MONDE

POUR GRACE UN VOILE DE MARIÉE

N 72 DU 31 MARS AU 7 AVR. ... NORD 60 FR. · MAROC 65 FR. · 10 FR. BELGES · 90 CENT. SUISSES · CANADA 25 C. · ITALIE 150 LIRES · ESPAGNE 12 PTAS 50 FR

3

one last reportage. It was a sublime wedding of which Grace Kelly would say that she hated every second. Hollywood never got over the loss. Grace dreamed of quietly starting a family, far from the public eye. But it was not to be. The paparazzi hounded Her Serene Highness with more determination than they had the movie star, despite her attempts to keep the press out of her private life. A perfectionist, she did her best to succeed at being the perfect princess, wife and mother. But despite her best efforts all three children grew up under the glare of flashbulbs.

Princess Beauty

As soon as she became a princess her husband forbade her to return to the Hollywood fold and banned the projection of her films in Monaco. However, the Monegasques soon took to crossing the border into France to admire their much-loved princess on the big screen. Her beauty lent a sparkle to the monarchy that it had never known. Thanks to her the world's press, purveyors of dreams, developed an interest in Monaco, bringing new life to the principality. But from the end of the 1960s Monaco encountered various political and financial problems while the royal couple started to fray. Leading separate lives in private, Grace and Rainier put up a good show when in public or on their palace balcony. Grace persevered in her charity work and in raising her tumultuous children who were particularly difficult to manage since they were always in the papers.

On the 13th of September 1982, while driving her daughter Stéphanie back to the palace, she lost control of her car which careered into a ravine. The gutter press noted that the accident took place at the exact spot where she had shot a scene with Cary Grant in *To Catch a Thief* thirty years before. She died the next day.

1. *Paris Match*. Photo, G. Lukomsky, 17th November 1959.
2. *Paris Match*. 17th March 1956. 3. *Jours de France*. 31st March to 7th April 1956.

The Family

The fascination with the Kennedys is the fascination with the American Dream. The story starts in 1849 when Patrick, the President's grandfather, arrived from Ireland. It was his son Joseph who amassed the considerable family fortune, through mostly illicit activities, before going into politics.

Appointed ambassador to London by Franklin Roosevelt, Joseph's isolationist views prevented him from climbing any higher. It would be up to his eldest son Joe to fulfil his father's presidential ambitions.

However, Joe was killed during the war and it fell to his younger brother John Fitzgerald (known as Jack), to take up the torch.

The American Dream

JFK was young, intelligent and charismatic, with a ravishing wife and beautiful children. In short, he was perfect material for magazine covers. When he ran as the Democratic candidate for President in 1960, his campaign was managed by his equally brilliant brother Robert.

Hs victory was the height of both the American dream and the Kennedy family. For the first time, the press gave as much space to the President's family as they did to the President himself. Given the press's infatuation, the Bay of Pigs débâcle was soon forgotten and blind eyes were turned as America became embroiled in Vietnam.

The dream unravelled with the assassination of JFK in 1963. When it was predicted that the third son Robert (known as Bobby) would win the 1968 presidential elections, a Kennedy dynasty in the White House seemed more than likely (8). But the American dream had been superseded by violence and, with 500,000 GIs stuck in Vietnam, Robert was in turn assassinated before the elections.

As the country changed, the dream became less and less American with conservative trends taking back the field from the Kennedys' liberal stance. Although Joe's fourth son Edward (known as Ted) is still a Senator from Massachusetts, the Kennedy name has slipped from the political pages and these days is seen more in the gossip columns.

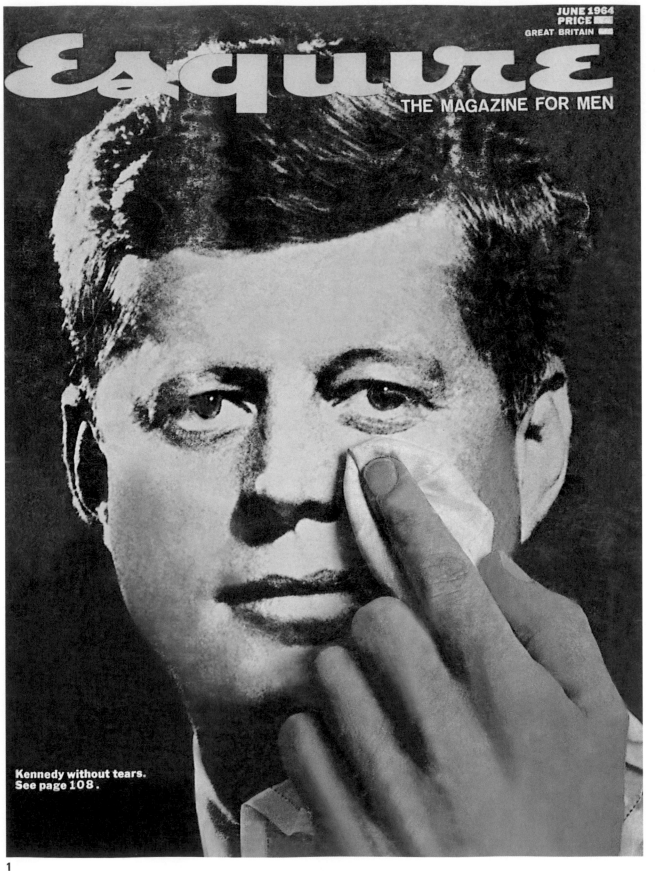

JUNE 1964
PRICE
GREAT BRITAIN

Esquire
THE MAGAZINE FOR MEN

Kennedy without tears.
See page 108.

1

2

3

4

5

6

7

8

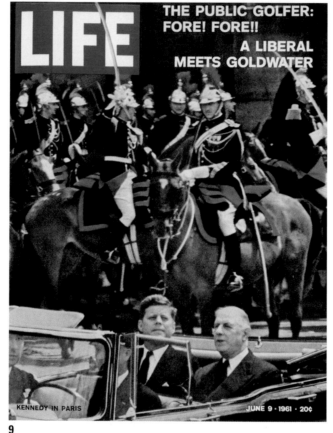

9

1. *Esquire.* Photo, Carl Fischer. Design, George Lois, June 1964. 2. *Life.* Photo, Nina Leen, 21st April 1958. Art Director, Charles Tudor. 3. *Life.* Photo, Leonard McCombe, 27th January 1961. Art Director, Charles Tudor. 4. *Life.* Photo, Stanley Tretick/UPI, 19th December 1960. Art Director, Charles Tudor. 5. *Life.* Photo, Paul Schutzer, 21st November 1960. Art Director, Charles Tudor. 6. *Life.* Photo, Mark Shaw, 1st September 1961. Art director, Charles Tudor. 7. *Life.* Photo, George Silk, 3rd July 1964. Art Director, Bernard Quint. 8. *Esquire.* Photo, Carl Fischer. Design, George Lois, April 1967. Art Director, Samuel N. Antupit. 9. *Life.* Photo, John Schutzer, 9th June 1961. Art Director, Charles Tudor. 10. *Life.* Photo, George Silk, 29th May 1964. Art Director, Bernard Quint. 11. *Life.* Photo, Bert and Richard Morgan Studio, 26th April 1963. Art Director, Bernard Quint. 12. *Life.* Photo, Walter Daran, 2nd October 1964. Art Director, Bernard Quint. 13. *Life.* Photo, Leonard McCombe, 15th January 1965. Art Director, Bernard Quint. 14. *Newsweek.* 1st January 1962. 15. *Life.* Photo, Karsh/Pix, 4th August 1961. Art Director, Charles Tudor.

10

11

12

13

14

15

The Human Face of Communism?

When Stalin died in 1953 the whole world held its breath and wondered who would succeed him. This was the iciest period of the cold war. The world was split in two.

Only the communist press spoke out in favour of the USSR. The Soviet dignitaries who attended the funeral of the dictator, with their ill fitting suits and easily identifiable hats were cause for concern rather than hope.

Several months later, Nikita Khrushchev emerged as the victor of the internal power struggle and was appointed First Secretary of the Communist Party. The new strong man of Russia was virtually an unknown. The western press had great difficulty in obtaining decent photographs of him that had not been doctored by the Soviet press corps (6).

Sitting comfortably on the further side of sixty, as broad as he was tall, Nikita Krushchev had a chubby face and a murky past. After the war he had personally masterminded the purge of the Ukraine. Stalin accused the region of favouring the Nazis and after the war he ordered thousands of executions and hundreds of thousands of deportations to the gulags.

The Thaw

But despite his past it was Krushchev who denounced Stalin's crimes in a seven hour speech to the 20th Party Congress, concluding thus: 'Let us swear to abolish the personality cult forever'.

But the personality cult simply shifted focus, with Stalin's portraits being replaced in the Soviet press by those of Krushchev. Still, Krushchev did make a change in oratory, doing away with the reading of long, boring and predictable speeches. This change of style won him many admirers in the West.

1. *L'Express.* Photo, Reporters Associés, 19th to 25th October 1964. Art Director, André Gobert. 2. *Der Spiegel.* 17th July 1957. 3. *Life.* Photo, Hank Walker, 5th October 1959. Art Director, Charles Tudor. 4. *Look.* Photo, Frank Bauman, 19th November 1963. Art Director, Philip Sykes and Joseph Tarallo. 5. *Life.* Photo, Karsh, 4th December 1970. Art Director, Irwin Glusker. 6. *Jours de France.* 17th to 24th February 1955.

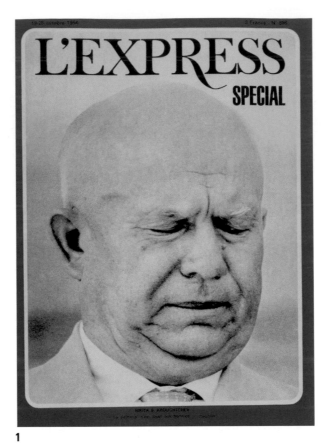

1

2

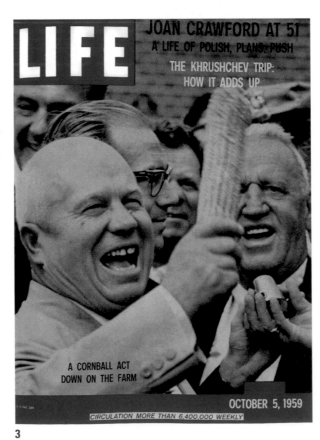

3

LIFE

KHRUSHCHEV REMEMBERS WORLD WAR II

The great battles

His fear of execution

Stalin's cowardice

KHRUSHCHEV
1963 portrait
by Karsh

DECEMBER 4 · 1970 · 50¢

Shifting from bonhomie to anger in an instant, Krushchev's histrionics rendered him much more human. With the launch of Sputnik in 1957 which humiliated America, the prestige of the USSR was re-established and the repression of the Hungarian insurrection of the previous year soon forgotten.

1960: Krushchev Peaks and then Declines

In 1960 Khrushchev felt sufficiently confident to get himself invited to the United States. This was the first time that a Soviet leader had visited the West. Standing next to the old and stuffy President Eisenhower, the vitality and charm of 'Mr Niet', as he was nicknamed, did wonders for his image in the American press.

This marked the peak of Krushchev's profile in the media. His decline started the very same year during a memorable visit to the U.N., where his incessant and spectacular interruptions of each and every speaker whose views differed from his own revealed his totalitarian nature and that of the regime he represented. Banging his shoe in an attempt to silence his detractors, Krushchev lost the very propaganda battle he had come to fight.

JOURS de FRANCE

KHROUCHTCHEV
le nouveau maître
de la Russie

PARTICIPEZ A NOTRE
GRAND CONCOURS
POUR TOUS LES AGES

N° 15   50f

6

A Photographer's Dream

In 1991 Sophia Loren received an Oscar for her lifetime achievements. On that night she was described as 'one of the most authentic treasures in cinema'. She had finally garnered the unanimous support of critics and the public. Yet the relationship between the actress from Pozzuoli, near Naples, and the international press had not always been so idyllic. The newspapers threw themselves at her, painting a picture of an arriviste who always used her body to win over the public. The difficulties of a childhood in her native village of Pozzuoli, devastated by the war, doubtless explain much about the character of this actress, considered offhand and unscrupulous.

Provocative and Bewitching

As a child Sophia Scicolone dreamed of the cinema. But her débuts at Cinecittà in 1949 were not that promising. Her provocative appearance distracted critics from the artistic qualities that she demonstrated in her all too brief appearances. In *Aida,* she was given her first leading role, playing the Ethiopian princess. The press started to recognise a certain professionalism in her.

But her credibility as an actress was eclipsed by the sex-symbol image that would haunt her throughout her life. It is nevertheless true that a clearly magnetic force emanated from a 'face and a body to damn all the saints in paradise', as a journalist for the *New York Times* wrote in 1953. Such beauty bewitched the producer Carlo Ponti, who became both her husband and her guiding star in the world of the seventh art.

The Gold of Naples marked her entry into the neo-realist cinema of Vittorio De Sica. Playing the role of a seductive pizza maker, she personifies 'the typical Neapolitan swagger, blood boiling as fiercely as the fire of Vesuvius'. 'Miss Loren – added a journalist from the New York *Times* – is clever, sarcastic and full of pride. The conquering air she adopts before her husband's clients is a work of art and cunning.' It was the start of the success which would see her play opposite De Sica in several seductress roles, as in *Scandal in Sorrento,* although her sensuality scandalised the more

1

2

3

4

6

7

8

Catholic critics, who considered her plunging necklines to be immoral.

The Pizzaiola

The 'pizzaiola' was what the newspapers now called Sophia Loren: passionate, sensual and sunny as they imagined the women of Naples to be. The leap from Naples to Hollywood would be risky for many. In the eyes of the critics, the 'Neapolitan' was only a caricature next to the behemoths of American cinema like Cary Grant, Gary Cooper or John Wayne. Now it was her accent that was criticised by the press. But after a tricky start, the newspapers had to acknowledge the multifaceted talent of this stunningly beautiful actress. Upon her return to Italy she co-starred in several films with Marcello Mastroianni including *Yesterday, Today and Tomorrow; Marriage Italian-style; A Special Day.* And it was in an Italian film that she reached the peak of her career, playing the title role in *La Ciociara* (Two Women) in 1961, winning an Oscar for Best Actress, as well as the Best Actress prize at Cannes. Admired both as an actress and as a woman of great class, she never stopped surprising the critics.
'A truly marvellous women with eternal beauty', declared *People Magazine.* Marcello Mastroianni, her most faithful co-star, would certainly have agreed with her when, in the film *Prêt-à-porter* (1994), Sophia Loren repeated the striptease that had made her famous forty years before.

1. *Der Stern.* 1957. **2.** *Stern.* 1964. **3.** *Life.* Photo, Leonard McCombe, 6th May 1957. Art Director, Charles Tudor. **4.** *Sunday Telegraph Magazine.* 12th November 1978. **5.** *Epoca.* 11th May 1958. Art Director, Alberto Guerri. **6.** *Paris Match.* Photo, Patrice Habans, 23rd February 1963. **7.** *Life.* Photo, Eric Schultness/B. S. Paramount Pictures, 14th November 1960. Art Director, Charles Tudor. **8.** *Paris Match.* Photo, François Pagès, 11th June 1960.

Sexy Chameleon

I f ever there was a star who knew how to use the media as much as the media used her, then it was definitely Madonna, the queen of carefully engineered scandal, first a dancer, then a successful singer, occasionally an actress and always a fearsome businesswoman.

Born in Michigan in 1958 to a family of eight children, she lost her mother when she was six. Sent to a Catholic boarding school, she had a burning ambition to be somebody. She convinced a DJ friend to play one of her tunes, *Everybody*, in the disco where he spun records. This first successful contact with the public encouraged her to send her demos to the Sire record label, who gave Madonna her first contract. Her third single, *Holiday,* released in 1984, was a massive hit.

Storming Success Story

Her first album, *Madonna,* stayed in the American Top 100 for 36 weeks. The same year, *Like A Virgin* surpassed the most optimistic predictions, selling 7 million in the United States! In just a year she had become a superstar. The six thousand tickets for her Los Angeles concert in 1985 sold out in just a few hours, leaving 100,000 empty-handed fans wishing they'd been quicker off the mark. In May 1985 she made the cover of *Time* magazine. More than just a singer, Madonna was a true social phenomenon. Bare midriff, fishnet stockings, underwear worn over her clothes (or thrown to the crowd), wildly styled hair, kitsch jewellery and oversized crucifixes created a new look, part punk, part whore, setting fashion trends for a whole generation. Unlike many stars for whom the sudden thrust into the celebrity spotlight left them vulnerable and fragile, Madonna took it all on the chin, coolly directing every step of her career, perfectly embodying the enterprising spirit of the 1980s. *Playboy* and *Penthouse* both published stills from an erotic film she had made in her youth, but since Madonna herself thrived on scandal it only served to boost her image.

Devil or Angel

Perhaps the key to her success was the paradox that she cultivated: icon and iconoclast,

1

2

3

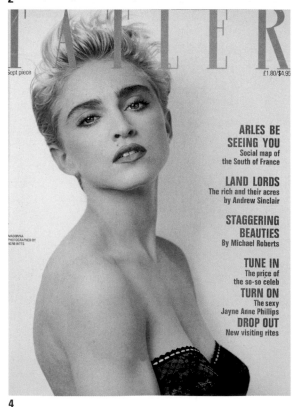

4

THE FACE

No 33/JUNE 1991 £1.50 • US $4.95
ITALY L6000 GERMANY 8.90DM SPAIN 435PTAS BELG. 202BFR

MADONNA
photographed by
Steven Meisel

EMF
New brats on
the block

**JODIE
FOSTER**
on female heroes

Paul Weller
Ninjaman • Omar
De Niro & the Red Scare
MOO! How James, Carter,
Ned's and Inspirals make
money on your backs

IN BED WITH
MADONNA
THE INSIDE STORY

9 770263 121002

doll and dominatrix, power woman and lithe romantic. *Like A Virgin* (1984) sold 9 million discs. Her changing looks and lovers provided ample copy for magazines. *True Blue* (1986) gave her a tougher, leaner image before the innocent young girl of *Papa Don't Preach* (1986), while *La Isla Bonita* (1987) was a true summer hit. During her long *Who's That Girl* tour of 1987, she switched direction once more, transforming herself into a glamour queen, a new platinum blonde Marilyn gracing the covers of *Life* and *Vanity Fair*. Two years later, just when it was thought that she had become well-behaved, she released *Like A Prayer* with its video clip containing black Christ figures and scandalous imagery.

At the same time, her film appearances and boisterous private life, including her marriage to the actor Sean Penn and the daughter she named Lourdes, helped to maintain the image of a character that could never be pinned down. In 1990 she undertook a year-long world tour, the *Blond Ambition* Tour, during which the documentary *In Bed With Madonna* was made. At its London première the guests were invited to attend wearing their night-clothes… The same year the video of *Justify My Love* with Lenny Kravitz was banned.

Alternating facile provocation (publication of her book *Sex* in 1992) with attempts to make her name as a serious actress (she played the role of Eva Perón, the Argentine heroine in Alan Parker's film of Andrew Lloyd Webber's *Evita*), she nevertheless continued her singing career, embracing the latest trends, surrounding herself with the best people and revealing not only an iron will in that silky body but also an unmistakable flair.

1. *Stern*. 1992. 2. *A les Aventures de l'Art*. Cover, Frida Kahlo, March 1991. Art Director, Michel Assouline. 3. *Punch*. 13th July 1990. 4. *Tatler*. Photo, Herb Ritts. 5. *The Face*. Photo, Steven Meisel, June 1991.

Utopia and Barbarism

Mao Tse-Tung was undoubtedly the man who gave China the unity and force necessary to hew a place for itself in the world worthy of its economic and demographic power.

Yet the image of Mao and Maoism in the Western press of the period was by and large an inaccurate one. The lack of information, the complexity of the situation under a regime where secrecy was enshrined at the highest level and a subtle propaganda that deceived many were the main reasons. From 1949 to 1976 Mao was the object of a personality cult so vast that only the intensity of certain periods enabled specialists to guess his true power. For although China was finally at peace, Mao was locked in a permanent struggle with his rivals.

Ignorance and Complacency

Around 1957 China was threatened by the de-Stalinisation of its Soviet neighbour. Having supported Stalin, China needed to mark its distance from the Soviet Union. Although China had gained its independence it had lost 15 million of its inhabitants in the famine caused by the failure of the Great Leap Forward, an absurd economic programme intended primarily to reinforce the power of the Great Helmsman, as Mao styled himself. Pushed to the sidelines he retook the offensive in 1965-1969. Accusing his enemies of revisionism he triggered the Cultural Revolution. In their quest to create The New Man, thousands of fanatical students, the Red Guards, undertook a reign of terror, suppressing all symbols of the past and of Mao's adversaries. Mao hung on to power until his death in 1976. Two years later Deng Xiaoping, the new leader, officially launched the process of de-Maoisation (4).

In the West, the press rarely got a grip on the reality of what was happening in China and often judged Mao with certain ideological preconceptions. Only the American press (3) truly questioned the situation in China. The French Communist magazine *Regards* provides a good example of this personality cult in its 1958 issues (6). Just two years later there would be a clear break and Mao would

2

3

4

5

6

disappear from its pages. This exclusion of Mao from official Communism on the part of Moscow only served to benefit him, since he could now claim to be a representative of the Third World, pressing for general revolution and guerrilla warfare. A section of the French Left in 1968, refusing what they perceived as the petit bourgeois communism of Soviet Russia, paraded carrying Mao's Little Red Book. The ultimate example of his personality cult, nearly a billion copies were reportedly printed of this little book. But there was a huge gulf between the Cultural Revolution pursued by the Chinese students and the wild fantasies of the French Maoist students of 1968. The *Magazine Littéraire* (5) believed in the 'cultural' version of what was nothing but a struggle between rival factions of the Chinese Communist Party.

1. *Paris Match.* 18th September 1976. **2.** *Stern.* 1965. **3.** *Newsweek.* Photo, Magnum, 25th November 1963. Art Director, Alfred Lowry. **4.** *Figaro magazine.* Cover, Marcel Laverdet, 4th November 1978. **5.** *Magazine littéraire.* Photo, Keystone, July 1969. **6.** *Regards.* December 1958.

The Most Photographed Woman in the World

The first time that Norma Jean Mortenson appeared on the cover of a magazine she was nineteen years old, a brunette and working in a parachute factory. An army photographer chose her to illustrate an issue devoted to women participating in the war effort. On the 26th of June 1945 she made the cover of *Fank,* followed by dozens of other magazines. Her beauty had clearly struck a chord with more than one art director. With her mother interned in a psychiatric hospital and never having known her own father, she dreamt of having one like Clark Gable. She devoured images of the stars whose ranks she desperately wanted to join.

Miss Golden Dreams

Encouraged by her first modelling success she joined the Blue Book agency before being contracted by 20th Century Fox as an actress. She changed her name and hair colour. A sex symbol was born. Photographers were quick to realise that they were dealing with someone exceptionally photogenic. To get a little extra cash, Marilyn posed nude for a calendar entitled Miss Golden Dreams. Fox demanded that she deny it was her. Marilyn refused and publicly admitted it saying: 'I needed the money, so I did it'. Her sincerity won her the hearts of the public. The calendar, suitably retouched, sold all over the world. Her victory was celebrated by a *Life* cover dedicated to her on the 7th of April 1952.

Marilyn became a Hollywood star with *Niagara,* followed by *Gentlemen Prefer Blondes.* Each month Fox received a torrent of requests for photographs. In 1954 Marilyn married the baseball champion Joe DiMaggio. 'The union of two living legends' headlined the world's press. During her honeymoon she made morale-boosting visits to American soldiers engaged in the Korean War. She appeared so often on the cover of the army magazine *Stars and Stripes* that they even published the same photo of her twice. Her diaphanous skin, curves and extreme seductiveness delighted photographers everywhere. The many photo sessions that she accorded magazines were

1

2

3

4

5

often fun occasions. When she shot the famous scene in *The Seven Year Itch* where she walks over the subway grate, photographers and fans jostled for a glimpse. Everywhere she went, even Japan, she caused a huge stir.

Sex Symbol of the 20th Century

When she divorced from DiMaggio, who was mad with jealousy, she received two hundred and fifty marriage proposals a week. Yet Marilyn suffered deeply from being considered just a tasty pin-up. She longed to be taken seriously as an actress. But the press was tough and laughed at such ambitions. *Life* magazine even qualified such desires as 'irrational', while *Time* declared that 'her acting talent, if she has any, is second to her most authentic gift, her steamy, come hither gaze'. In 1955 she took classes at the Actors Studio to hone her acting skills. When she married the playwright Arthur Miller, the press proved themselves to be true champions of vulgarity, headlining 'the marriage of the intellectual and the brainless star'. Her alleged affair with President Kennedy only added to her aura. Theories abound as to the circumstances of her death. Was she a victim of her success, succombing to depression and drugs, or was there some sinister plot? The enigma remains unanswered. 'I don't care about the money,' she said. 'I just want to be fabulous.'

1. *Life*. Photo, Philippe Halsman, 9th November 1959. Art Director, Charles Tudor. 2. *Paris Match*. 18th to 25th July 1953. 3. *Le Nouveau F.* July-August 1982. Art Director, Gérard Suner. 4. *Sunday Telegraph Magazine*. 1st March 1981. 5. *The Sunday Times Magazine*. 22nd July 2001.

Overleaf
6. *The Sunday Times Magazine*. 7th October 1973. 7. *The Sunday Times Magazine*. 16th September 1973. 8. *Sunday Telegraph Magazine*. 22nd July 1984. 9. *Stern*. 1966.

THE SUNDAY TIMES *magazine*
MARILYN-
THE LAST DAYS
OCTOBER 7, 1973

6

THE SUNDAY TIMES *magazine*
SEPTEMBER 16, 1973

MARILYN MONROE
NORMAN MAILER

7

TELEGRAPH

SUNDAY MAGAZINE

Number 404 July 22 1984

Exclusive

THE YOUNG MARILYN

Unpublished photographs of Marilyn Monroe at the start of her career

9

deshalb mußte Marilyn Monroe sterben

Glücklich in der DDR

Geishas küssen auch

Keine Angst vor Depressionen

Overleaf
Marilyn covers from all over the world.

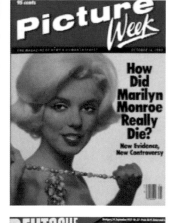

Carnival Caesar

The reign of Mussolini and Fascism lasted nearly 23 years, twice as long as that of Hitler and Nazism. Over the years, the press scrutinised Mussolini and portrayed the phenomenon in various ways.

At first the movement and its leader succeeded in winning hearts and minds through its dynamism and originality. But reality then impinged and revealed the illusion. Under the influence of the even more dangerous Hitler, Il Duce revealed his criminal yet farcical nature. Yet when he took power Mussolini gave the image of a charismatic leader. He created a personality cult that fitted the fascist ideology perfectly, characterised by the supposedly virile power that he emanated. The press was full of exhibitionist photographs (3) showing him stripped to the waist skiing, threshing corn with the peasants or leading a sporting event with his ministers.

One of Il Duce's successes seized upon by the press was his conciliation with the pope (2) and the creation of the Vatican State. To earn what appeared in the eyes of the Catholic population to be a papal blessing, Benito

1

LE PAPE OU LE DUCE?

Le conflit entre le catholicisme et le fascisme est, paraît-il, en voie de règlement. Il n'en est pas moins symptomatique pour notre époque, que les pouvoirs temporels et spirituels, qui ont récemment signé un concordat et un traité liquidant les anciens litiges, en arrivent à une collision brutale. Et pourtant, ne se ressemblent-ils pas, quel que soit l'esprit qui les anime, les gestes de ces deux meneurs d'hommes : la bénédiction du pape et le salut du duce?

PARAIT LE MERCREDI
4ᵉ ANNÉE -- N° 170

Directeur : Lucien VOGEL

17 JUIN 1931
PRIX : 2 FRANCS

2

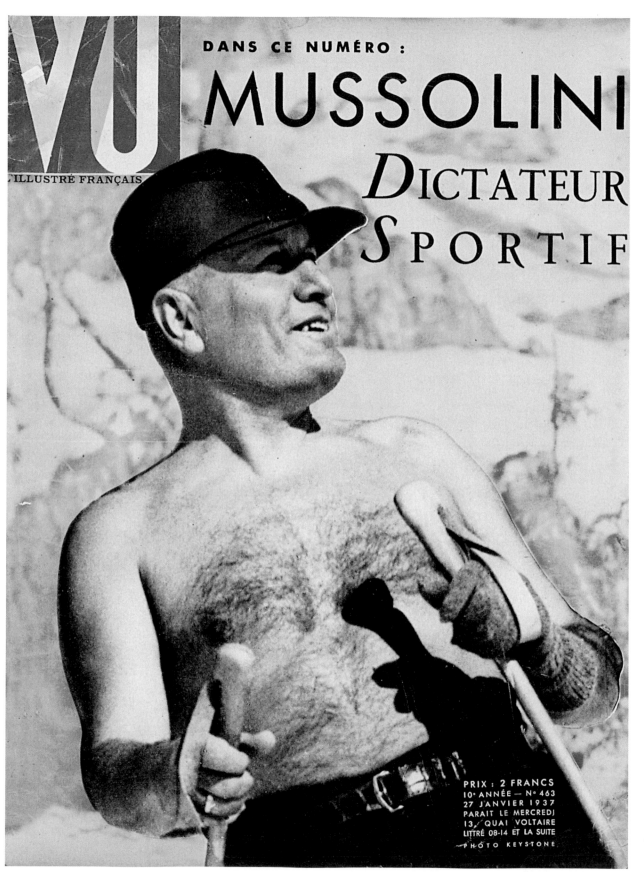

4

Mussolini momentarily abandoned his extreme anticlericalism.

Decline and Fall

But 'the man who made the trains run on time' and who had provided the Nazis with their fascist model quickly took second place to Hitler. Nazism copied both the Roman salute (2) and marching step (4). Over time Mussolini's brilliant speeches revealed themselves to be the bully-boy boastings that they were. The true face of Mussolini is that of the cover of *Time* June 1941 (1). His army had failed in all of the military operations it had undertaken. The Werhmacht was now fighting for Mussolini, extracting him from brief detention in 1943 in a daring commando mission, and he was disguised as a German soldier when he was recaptured and shot in 1945.

1. *Time*. Cover, Ernest Hamlin Baker, 9th June 1941. 2. *Vu*. 17th June 1931. 3. *Vu*. Photo, Keystone, 27th January 1937. 4. *Le Rire*. Cover, Paul Ordner, 18th February 1938.

Mysterious Personality Cult

Until quite recently, Stalin was a controversial figure. Contrary to Hitler, who was unequivocally demonised, both public opinion and the press have held varying images of Stalin, though there were more similarities than differences between the two dictators.

An Ambiguous Image

From Stalin's rise to power in 1928 until his death in 1953, the press expressed their widely varied opinions of him. This was the result of several factors. The view of politics as drama and the rise of extremists meant that more than ever the press served to voice opinions rather than provide objective information. There were also the great practical difficulties of checking the veracity of information coming out of the USSR, not to mention that country's powerful propaganda and disinformation machine. This all resulted in a press and a world that was split between pro and anti-Stalin camps.

Man of the Year? Man of Peace?

The cover of *Regards* (4) resembles any journal of the period. Only when reading it does one

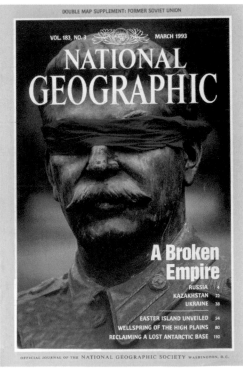

1

2

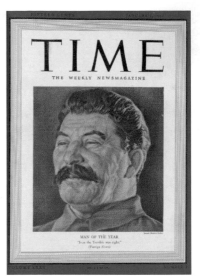

4

5

70ᵗᴴᴱ ANNIVERSAIRE DE
STALINE
L'HOMME DE LA PAIX

FRANCE-URSS   DÉCEMBRE 1949   N° 52   PRIX

3

discover its views. *Photo Monde* (2) takes an ironic anti-communist stance by attempting to trivialise him like some film star. Meanwhile Stalin was orchestrating policies that resulted in famine and millions of deaths. The reality of Soviet Russia was much bleaker than that suggested by these magazines, but there were neither photographs nor eyewitness accounts to prove it. And when occasional rumours did emanate from Russia there was often an unwillingness to believe them. Was this not the Worker's Paradise after all? In 1949, fear of a nuclear holocaust might explain the Man of Peace title conferred by the communist journal *France-URSS* (3) on Stalin, who was celebrating his 70ᵗʰ birthday. The photograph itself is either old or airbrushed, since the man looks twenty years younger. Such was his personality cult. The Man of the Year 1940 photo that appeared on the cover of *Time* (5) shows Stalin's slightly Asian features well. Even at the fall of the Soviet empire and 40 years after his death (1), the legacy of the man who insisted that Ivan the Terrible was right was still a powerful one.
But has Stalin's statue been blindfolded to suggest a man about to be shot, or so that he should not see the collapse of his empire?

1. *National Geographic.* Cover, Gerd Ludwig, March 1993. Art Director, Allen Carroll.
2. *Photo Monde.* 18ᵗʰ March 1933. 3. *France-URSS.* December 1949. 4. *Regards.*
October 1952. 5. *Time.* Cover, Ernest Hamlin Baker, 1ˢᵗ January 1940.

A Picture is Worth a Thousand Words

Napoléon once said that a drawing was worth more than a long speech. Caricaturists and illustrators both know this for fact, as do magazine editors. In many cases a person's photograph suggests a particular perception of them. Sometimes a little staging is necessary but a talented photographer will often be able to capture a person's pose at exactly the right moment.

The photographs of Freud (1) and Hitchcock (7) are particularly significant. The inventor of psychoanalysis is pictured staring at a sculpture of his own head, confronted with himself, his own conscious and subconscious. And you do not have to read the table of contents of *Life* to realise that Alfred Hitchcock is promoting his new film *The Birds*.

The photograph of Louis Armstrong (10) requires no explanation. The way the picture itself has been taken, with the trumpet thrust towards the lens to create a magnified effect, tells the whole story. Albert Einstein (4) needs no particular staging. The simple act of sticking out his tongue shows that there is no contradiction between genius and a sense of humour.

Religious Icon – the Pope

John Paul II (3), *Time* magazine's man of the year for 1994, is depicted as a Renaissance fresco. The pope who would leave the greatest mark on the 20th century is here thought worthy of being immortalised in the same way his Renaissance predecessors were.

Secular Icon – Che Guevara

Taken in 1960, the famous photograph by the Cuban Alberto Korda appeared just a few weeks after the death of the Marxist hero in 1967. It has been reproduced in all kinds of media imaginable, from students' posters to murals, T-shirts and Cuban banknotes. However, when a major commercial vodka manufacturer attempted to use the image for promotional purposes, Korda took them to court in London and won. This image of Che (8) has stood the test of time. Snapped in his youth for eternity, Che represents the hopes of the Revolution. But the image of the other

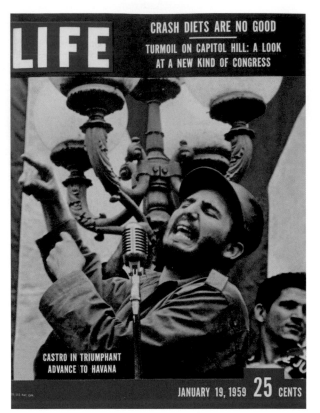

1

2

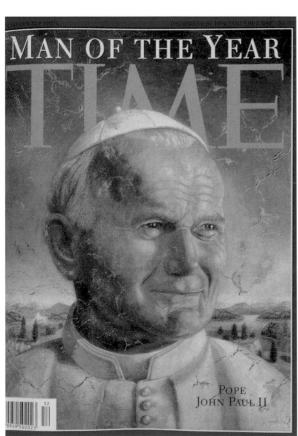

3

4

5

6

7

8

hero of the Cuban revolution, Fidel Castro (2), has not reached such iconographic status, probably because he is still alive. At 33 years old in this photo from 1959, Fidel is the same age as Che. But today the beard is now grey and the five-hour speeches out of vogue. The longest ruling dictator in the world, a thorn in the side of the USA who has clung onto power in a poverty-stricken nation and is rather less of a role model than he once was.

Elder Statesmen

Other old hands of the world stage are treated with a little more ambiguity. At 81 years old, the founder of the Federal Republic of Germany, Konrad Adenauer, had been Chancellor for 8 years when this edition of *Der Spiegel* (6) appeared. This black and white portrait, accentuating his drawn features, seems to suggest that it is perhaps time to hand over the reins. But his successors would have to wait another 6 years before he took well-earned retirement. Hô Chi Minh (5) at 69 years old and president of North Vietnam looks fit as a fiddle, just like his army that so effectively resisted the American colossus. But Uncle Ho would die the following year and so would not see his country reunified five years later.

Singers Old and Young

Elvis would be 67 today. But we remember the youthful features of the 1950s (9) rather than the obesity of the 1970s. And what face will Michael Jackson (11) have at 67?

1. *Vu.* Sigmund Freud. 20th July 1932. 2. *Life.* Fidel Castro. Cover, Andrew St George, 19th January 1959. Art Director, Charles Tudor. 3. *Time.* John Paul II. Fresco, Richard Selesnick and Nicolas Kalin. Photo, Robert Ammirati, 26th December 1994 to 2nd January 1995. Art Director, Arthur Hochstein. 4. *Semaine du Monde.* Albert Einstein. 23rd May 1953. 5. *Life.* Hô Chi Minh. Cover, Charles Bonnay/Black Star, 22nd March 1968. Art Director, Bernard Quint. 6. *Der Spiegel.* Conrad Adenauer. 11th September 1957. 7. *Life.* Alfred Hitchcock. Cover, Philippe Halsman, 1st February 1963. Art Director, Bernard Quint. 8. *Evergreen.* Che Guevara. Cover, Paul Davis, February 1968. Art Director, Ken Deardoff.

Overleaf
9. *Rolling Stone.* Elvis Presley. 10. *Life.* Louis Armstrong. Cover, Philippe Halsman, 15th April 1966. Art Director, Bernard Quint. 11. *L'Écho des Savanes.* Michael Jackson. Cover, R.Corkery/Sygma, 7th to 13th September 1984. Art Director, Jean-Claude Barotto.

$1.00 UK50p

ROLLING STONE

ELVIS PRESLEY
1935-1977

LIFE

Louis
Armstrong

'I never did
want to be no
Big Star'

APRIL 15 · 1966 ·

PULL OUT CO

In an interview
with *RICHARD MERYMAN*
America's genius of jazz talks
his warm, intimate story—
from the golden boyhood days
in New Orleans to the fame
he didn't seek as Satchmo

l'Echo des Savanes

MICHAEL JACKSON
**DEHORS
LE FAUX
BLACK !**
PRINCE ARRIVE

**TESTEZ
VOTRE
PENIS**

REISER
PEPE
MORENO

11

The Star System

The first film posters to credit lead actors or actresses in 'starring roles' date from 1907-1908 in Europe. The United States proved to be much more hostile to this highly individual publicity. Actors remained virtually anonymous until the press took a hand, insisting that their readers' curiosity be satisfied and that the true names of Vitagraph Girl or Biograph Girl be revealed. In 1910 one audacious producer, Carl Laemmle of Biograph, created the first American film star, Florence Lawrence. There was no turning back.

The Race to Glory

During the 1920s young women flocked from all over Europe and America to try their luck in Hollywood. Daughters of workers (Greta Garbo), dentists (Jean Harlow), bankers (Shirley Temple) or boxers (Mae West), most of them had entered beauty or dance contests in which the first prize was a trip to cinema paradise. Treated as both goddesses and consumer goods, they let themselves be fashioned according to passing vogues and the various fantasies that their physiques suggested. They were living symbols of eternal femininity who served not only to fuel masculine dreams, but to provide examples of success

LIFE

THE GREAT GARBO
A CANDID BIOGRAPHY,
FIRST OF THREE PARTS

GARBO IN 1928, BY STEICHEN

20 CENTS

JANUARY 10, 1955

REG. U. S. PAT. OFF.

LIFE

LIFE AND WORK OF A DEBAUCHED GENIUS
THE INCREDIBLE MODIGLIANI
THE TENDERFOOT A-HUNTING GOES

CAT AND KIM NOVAK
IN FILM ABOUT WITCHES

NOVEMBER 24, 1958   25 CENTS

1

2

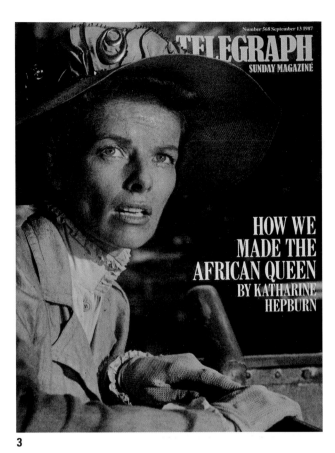

3

4

5

6

to the female readers who soon formed the majority of their audience, young emancipated urbanites vicariously living out their dreams on the silver screen. The stereotyping was unambiguous. There were the spruced up perfect homemakers (Mary Pickford, dubbed America's sweetheart), the sinful vamps (Theda Bara) or the saucy flapper girls of the Prohibition era.

The first fan clubs appeared during the 1920s, and specialist magazines developed, purveying fresh gossip to feed an obsessive public who were torn between idol worship and erotic adoration. It was not long before male actors were given the same treatment. The term Latin lover was invented specifically for Rudolf Valentino, an Italian émigré who became a world star, but it has long outlived him. He was at the height of his fame when he died in 1926. His funeral triggered scenes of hysteria and a number of women even committed suicide.

The Hollywood Firmament

The wind changed during the 1930s. The introduction of sound to cinema in 1927 put most stars of the silent era out of work, while the stock market crash of 1929 wiped the smile off many faces. But at the dream factory, production continued with Greta Garbo, Marlene Dietrich, Norma Shearer and Jean Harlow rivalling each other with their unattainable elegance. Three great genres of film became firmly established – screwball comedy, the gangster film and the melodrama – each with its coterie of female character types. There was something for everyone, from the deadly diva to the ideal or forsaken wife, the clever woman to the giggly but simple girl, the explosive pin-up to the inaccessible society lady. The birth of sound cinema also contributed to the democratisation of the image of the star. In 1935 authorisation was given to market the

1. *Life.* Kim Novak. Cover, Ralph Crane, 24th November 1958. Art director, Charles Tudor. 2. *Life.* Greta Garbo. Photo, Seichen, originally published October 1928 in *Vanity Fair.* Art director, Charles Tudor. 3. *Sunday Telegraph Magazine.* Katharine Hepburn. 13th September 1987. 4. *Picture Post.* Ingrid Bergman. 27th March 1943. 5. *Life.* Elizabeth Taylor. Cover, Howelle Conant/ 20th Century Fox, 6th October 1961. Art director, Bernard Quint. 6. *The Sunday Times Magazine.* Audrey Hepburn. 4th September 1966.

make-up used by the stars, previously considered to be professional secrets.

Demigods Like You and Me

After the Second World War, the ice-queen femme fatale of the 1940s gave way to family warmth and shapely figures.

In the 1950s an unforeseen adversary appeared that threatened to consign cinema to the attic of history. It was called television, and it created a new host of stars that were in tune with the times. The female stereotypes of the golden age of cinema now seemed rather dated and clichéd. Hollywood pulled out all the stops to fight the small screen. This was the era of super-productions, with big bucks, armfuls of stars, casts of thousands and new exciting technical advances including 3-D films, Technicolor and Cinemascope.

The public became younger, identifying with a new generation of rebels, led by James Dean and Marlon Brando. And it worked. Even after Hollywood buried James Dean in 1955 after his death in a car crash, 5 000 letters a day continued to be sent to him for several years. As for Marlon Brando, his star never lost its lustre, ushering in the era of the megastars in the 1970s when he was paid one million dollars for an appearance in *Superman* that lasted just ten minutes. But the prize for longevity surely goes to John Wayne, the definitive Hollywood cowboy, who stayed on top for thirty years.

How to Become a Star?

If over the course of the century cinema actors have gone from earning the right to have their name credited for a film to carrying a film on their name alone, the confusion between actor and character has never really ceased. To be considered a star, an actor or actress has to be sufficiently well known for their name to be intrinsically linked with a film. Since in the eyes of the adoring public all the films of a particular star form virtually a single movie, the star must be of a clearly recognisable type, enabling them to be easily identified from film to film. For an actor to become a legend they must repeatedly play roles that that have been proven to work best for them, with little variation: the heartbreaker (Rudolf Valentino), the disillusioned cynic (Humphrey Bogart), the lost adolescent

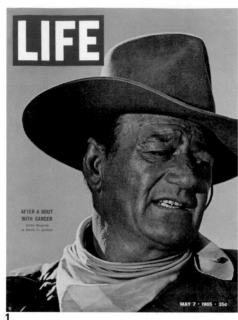

1

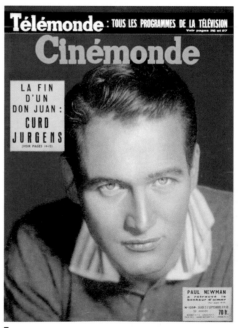

2

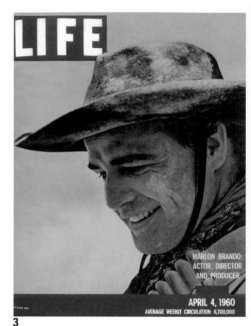

3

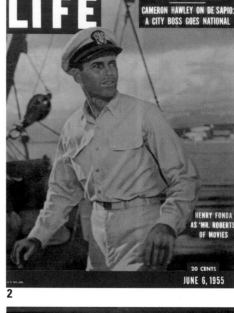

4

5

6

1. *Life.* John Wayne. Photo, John R. Hamilton/Globe, 7th May 1965. Art Director, Bernard Quint. 2. *Life.* Henry Fonda. Photo, Slim Aarons/Magnum, 6th June 1955. Art Director, Charles Tudor. 3. *Life.* Marlon Brando. Photo, Sam Shaw, 4th April 1960. Art Director, Charles Tudor. 4. *Life.* Gregory Peck. 20th February 1950. 5. *Cinémonde.* Paul Newman. 25th September 1958. 6. *Life.* Yul Brynner. Photo, Eric Carpenter/Magnum, 10th March 1958. Art Director, Charles Tudor. 7. *Paris Match.* Clark Gable. Photo, Henri Cartier-Bresson, 26th November 1960. 8. *Rolling Stone.* Robert Redford. 2nd October 1980.

8

(James Dean). To leave the security of one's typecast is playing with fire. Buster Keaton was bound by contract never to laugh in public, and when the publicity of the film *Ninotchka* proclaimed 'Garbo laughs!', she did not realise that she had ushered in retirement. Yet the Garbo myth endures, even for the masses of people who have never seen one of her films!

Collecting Stardust

The magazine press clearly found in the irresistible sparkle of these stars the material to entice a public hungry for images of their heroes. Seeing a famous face on a cover stirs feelings of both recognition and admiration. And because a magazine becomes a part of one's surroundings so readily, its effect is that much greater. You can swoon before stars like Paul Newman and Clark Gable on the silver screen then take them home on the cover of your favourite magazine.

NEWSPAPER AND MAGAZINE INDEX

BIOGRAPHICAL INDEX

Founders, editors, art directors, illustrators, artists, cartoonists, photographers, journalists and authors.

ACKNOWLEDGEMENTS

Our warmest thanks to La Galcante (les Temps de la Presse et de l'Image) and the American Library in Paris who were kind enough to open their doors to us, and without whom this book would never have appeared.

We would also like to thank: the editorial team of *Stern* magazine, particularly Mme Heidi Heuser, who provided us with the covers that appear in this book; Punch Cartoon Library and Archive, who gave us covers of *Punch* magazine; the Gamma agency, who made issues of *Paris Match* available to us; Fanny Bruno, who photographed the magazine covers that appear in this book; Noel Smart, who undertook research at the British Library.

Finally, thank you to Isabelle Bruneau, who helped research the images and collected all of the documentation.

The translator would like to thank Vincent Vichit-Vadakan for his assistance.

PHOTOGRAPHIC CREDITS

American Library in Paris: 10, 11, 12 (5), 16, 28-29, 32-37, 46-53, 68-69, 96 (3 and 5), 97, 98 (1), 99 (7 and 8), 100-101, 104 (12), 105 (16), 106 (1), 110-111, 120-123, 124 (4), 127 (5), 128 (1), 129 (7), 131 (2, 4 and 5), 132-134, 135 (2, 3 and 4), 141 (3), 145 (4 and 6), 152 (1), 153 (4), 154, 158-159, 160 (3), 161 (5), 162 (3), 163 (7), 167 (3), 168, 174 (1), 176 (1), 178 (2 and 3), 179 (5 and 7), 180 (10), 182, 183 (5), 184 (1, 2, 3, 4 and 6).

The British Library: 56-59, 66-67, 74-81, 95 (2), 125 (6), 127 (4), 141 (4 et 5), 142 (2 et 4), 143, 144, 145 (5), 146 (4), 148, 155 (3), 162 (4), 164 (4), 169 (4 et 5), 170, 171 (8), 180 (9), 183 (3, 4 et 6), 185 (8).

Gamma: 54-55, 105 (18), 129 (6), 136 (1), 137 (11), 138, 145 (7), 146 (1 et 3), 153 (5 et 6), 156, 163 (6 et 8), 166, 169 (2), 185 (7).

Punch Cartoon Library and Archive: 62-63, 94, 95 (5), 131 (3), 135 (5), 141 (2), 147 (12), 164 (3).

Sipa Press: 102 (6), 104 (11), 146 (2), 147 (5 à 11 et 13), 149.

Stern: 72-73, 95 (3), 99 (6), 102 (3), 104 (14), 105 (15), 142 (1), 150, 151 (2,3 et 5), 162 (1 et 2), 164 (1), 167 (2), 171 (9)

Les Temps de la Presse et de l'Image: 8, 12 (6, 7 et 8), 13, 14, 15, 17-19, 22-27, 30-31, 38-45, 60-61, 64-65, 70-71, 82-89, 92-93, 95 (4), 96 (1, 2 et 4), 98 (2, 3 et 4), 99 (5), 102 (1, 2, 4, 5 et 7), 103, 104 (13), 105 (17), 106 (2 à 4), 107, 108-109, 112-119, 124 (1 à 3), 125 (5), 126, 127 (6 à 8), 128 (2), 129 (3, 4, 5 et 8), 130, 136 (2), 137 (3 à 10), 139, 140, 142 (3), 145 (2 et 3), 151 (4, 6, 7 et 8), 152 (2 et 3), 155 (2, 4, 5 et 6), 157, 160 (1, 2 et 4), 161 (6), 163 (5), 164 (2), 165, 167 (4, 5 et 6), 169 (3), 174 (2), 175, 176 (2), 177, 178 (1 et 4), 179 (6 et 8), 181 (11), 184 (5).

D.R.: 172-173 and all of the reproductions from The American Library in Paris, The British Library, Gamma, Sipa and les Temps de la Presse et de l'Image.

Conceived and published by Copyright for Weidenfeld & Nicolson, based on an idea by Hervé Tardy
Graphic design: Yannick Le Bourg
Layout: Jacqueline Leymarie
Image research: Véronique Cardineau
Editorial co-ordination: Isabelle Raimond
English translation: Roland Glasser